SITUATION MOMEDY

A Very Special Episode in Toddlerdom

JENNA VON OY

MEDALLION

Medallion Press, Inc.

Printed in USA

Published 2017 by Medallion Press, Inc.
4222 Meridian Pkwy., Suite 110, Aurora, IL 60540

The MEDALLION PRESS LOGO
is a registered trademark of Medallion Press, Inc.

Copyright © 2017 by Jenna von Oy
Cover design by James Tampa
Cover photography by Brooke Boling

This work reflects the author's present recollections of specific experiences over a period of years. Dialogue and events have been recreated and in some cases compressed to convey the substance of what was said or what occurred. Some identifying details have been changed to protect the privacy of individuals.

Cataloging-in-Publication Data is on file with the Library of Congress

Typeset in Adobe Garamond Pro
Printed in the United States of America
ISBN 9781942546603

10 9 8 7 6 5 4 3 2 1
First Edition

DEDICATION

To my daughters, Gray and Marlowe. I don't possess words profound enough to express the depth of love I have for you, just a heart big enough to hold it all. You are everything I never knew I needed and more. It's a privilege to be your mommy.

And also to my husband, Brad. This wouldn't be the same book without you; you single-handedly saved the ending! More importantly, you gave me a beginning—the gift of a life with you and our two precious girls. You are one hell of a husband and father, and I love you.

To all the career-driven, stay-at-home, work-at-home, breastfeeding, formula-feeding, busting-your-ass-to-make-it-work-no-matter-what moms out there, regardless of your shape, size, age, race, religion, ethnicity, upbringing, political views, or social status. Thank you for continuing to inspire me to be the best mom I can be. You're the ones who make motherhood look good . . . I simply wrote a book about it.

Finally, in honor and loving memory of my sweet, special, beautiful boy, Bruiser, who gave me fifteen years of joy and pug kisses. Just as mommies come in all shapes and sizes, so do the babies we love and nurture. Sometimes those babies have paws instead of feet. You were, and always will be, my first baby and one of my greatest loves. You took a piece of me with you.

CONTENTS

"Driving" me crazy at Home Depot. *Photo courtesy of Jenna von Oy.*

PREFACE

If you've read my first book, *Situation Momedy: A First-Time Mom's Guide to Laughing Your Way through Pregnancy and Year One,* you're familiar with my tongue-in-cheek brand of parenting "advice." You probably also know I'm a mostly normal, relatively blunt, supersarcastic, slightly neurotic, often goofy, very long-winded former child star who's prone to drawn-out stories and self-deprecating humor. (Feel free to pity my husband.) You probably also know my favorite pastime (aside from getting a neck massage, while luxuriating in a bubble bath, while having a giant glass of cabernet sauvignon, while stuffing my face with chocolate cake, while daydreaming about Calvin Klein underwear models) is being a mommy.

If you're new to all of this, and you're just jumping on the *Momedy* bandwagon, I hope my take on motherhood makes you laugh until you cry. Actually, I hope I spare you the crying and instead inspire you to indulge in some therapy by chocolate. Or martinis. Or, better yet, chocolate martinis. Because I hate to break it to you, but those terrifically troublesome terrible twos will already be leaving enough tears in their wake, and I don't imagine you'll want to add to the mess. All I can say is drink responsibly—because you *will* drink. (My condolences if you live in a dry county or stolidly abstain. Quadruple that if it's because you're already pregnant with your next child, but I'll also throw in a "Congratulations!" along with it. See chapter 10 for more on that.)

I'm no pediatrician, baby-handling guru, or family shrink (God forbid!). What I *am* is a fellow mommy who believes in honesty and vulnerability when it comes to sharing my parenting experiences. I've found the less clinical approach to raising kids can be a welcome relief. Sometimes the most cherished and valuable assistance we receive during our happy-but-hectic journey is from our peers, because it reminds us to trust our own instincts and laugh our way through the most challenging moments. And by that I mean the moments when your kid is screaming so loud in front of a sea of total strangers you start thinking life might stink less if you were a dung beetle. My goal in all of this is to offer you a sense of empowerment and to encourage humor to prevail. When the going gets tough, the tough get to giggling! And possibly locking themselves in the bathroom for a rare thirty seconds of peace and quiet.

A Popsicle date with my beautiful, funny, wily toddlers.
Photo courtesy of Jenna von Oy.

I'm not here to overanalyze your parenting, judge your tactics and techniques, or gossip about you and your kid on social media. I'm here to wear my heart on my sleeve by offering insight into my own trials and tribulations, with the hope you might feel a little less alone out there in this mad, mad, Mommy War-torn world we live in.

The motherhood learning curve doesn't end after pregnancy and year one. Those stages are just the beginning of a very long, beautiful, educational adventure! We mommies might become a little less manic about pacifiers hitting the ground or a little more adept at recognizing the difference between teething sniffles versus those of a cold, but the grand tutorial has just begun. Toddlerdom is rife with struggles and satire too. You think sleep training was tough stuff? Wait until you're in the throes of potty training! It's a shit show, for real.

Parenthood is a work in progress, and we might as well continue forging ahead together. Who doesn't appreciate a little solidarity in the midst of the motherhood mania? In my first book we commiserated over pregnancy ailments and the joys of year one, such as the malodorous art of diaper changing, so why not share the anarchy and utter pandemonium of raising a child between the ages of one and four? It's frenzied. It's flabbergasting. It's freakin' fun.

Happy reading! I wish you continued comfort and pride in your parenting choices and endless humor to accompany them . . . because you're about to play a starring role in a very special episode in Toddlerdom.

Peace, Love, and Dirty Diapers,

A toddler strikes back . . . *Otherwise known as Gray locked me out of my cell phone again. Photo courtesy of Jenna von Oy.*

CHAPTER 1

Earning a Degree in Social Studies

A SCENIC VIEW OF MY PAST

I've spent the bulk of my adult career being a "Did I go to college with you?" kind of actress. I'm not offended; it comes with the territory. The truth is, I don't expect people to recognize me now, especially since most of my illustrious '90s character identifiers are gone. Contrary to my former alter ego, I'm a *non*-speed-talking (except after espresso), *non*-floppy-hat-wearing, Nashville-residing, married mommy of two. In fact, these days I'm more famous for being Gray and Marlowe's mom, and that's fine by me. It's *by far* the best title I've ever carried!

During the *Blossom* years, most sixteen-year-old girls in America could have easily picked me out of a police lineup. Thankfully, they never had to. Fans would approach me with more detailed knowledge of our episode story lines than I possessed, queries about how I managed to talk faster than a cattle auctioneer, and desperate requests for Joey Lawrence's private phone number. For the record, I'm not convinced he's ever actually trusted me with the real deal, so they were pleading a lost cause even if I'd been dumb enough to fork over his digits. Which I wasn't.

After *Blossom* went off the air in 1995 and syndication began to peter out, our legion of fans began to forget the context in which they'd seen my face. I became the frequent recipient of, "You were that chick on *Punky Brewster*, right?" Which was my favorite question just shy of, "Weren't you that whiny, annoying, wacky friend on *Full House*?" No, I was that *other* whiny, annoying, wacky best friend from the '90s.

When I hit my thirties, the questions evolved into "Do our kids go to the Rugrat Romper Room Academy together?" and "Don't you work at my gynecologist's office?" (You don't want me manning a speculum, I promise) and my favorite of all time: "Didn't I meet you last year at the Beer Pong World Series tournament?" Yes. Yes, you did.

It can be disorienting when non-actors see TV personalities out of context. I get a lot of blank stares, furrowed brows, and head scratching, as folks attempt to correctly tie a memory to that glimmer of recognition. I've gotten used to it, especially now that *Blossom* is back in syndication here and there. Don't feel embarrassed, for example, if we meet on the street and you mistake me for LeAnn Rimes or for your husband's vile ex-girlfriend. It won't be the first time for either of those scenarios. If it makes you feel any better, that sort of blunder isn't limited to those outside the entertainment industry. They also happen to insider folks who probably ought to put two and two together faster than you can get through a Saturday morning line at Costco.

When I was on *The Parkers*, we used to conduct post-taping cast and crew gatherings at a bar next to our studio lot. It was an opportunity for us to let off steam, rejoice in the blessing of a consistent gig, celebrate another week of making our audience laugh, and drink to forget the jokes that *failed* to make them laugh. Which sometimes required a few extra cocktails. Let's just say I knew the number to the local taxi service by heart.

One evening, our typical *Parkers* crowd was joined by one of the actresses who'd been recurring on our show, and we happened to say our good-byes at the same time. On our way out, I noticed a smattering of other prime-time sitcom casts. Apparently, we weren't the only ones with an after-show ritual to drink away the slapstick.

While waiting at the valet kiosk, my costar spotted another actress she'd worked with.

"I'm going to say hello," she informed me. I watched as she made her way over to a slender woman I recognized immediately, who was in midconversation with a group of friends and coworkers.

My costar patiently waited for an opportunity to catch up on old times.

"It's good to see you again," she finally interjected. "I'm sorry I don't remember your name, but I know you were a guest star on the UPN show I did a few years back."

"I don't think so," the other actress politely and graciously responded.

Her denial had zero effect on my costar, who kept pressing the issue. "No, I'm sure of it. Don't you remember? You had a bit part on my show, *Homeboys in Outer Space.*"

A bemused expression crept onto the woman's face, and her coworkers conspicuously stifled laughter. I cringed as I realized the confusion . . . My friend had watched *Frasier* so many times that she was mistaking Peri Gilpin for someone she'd worked with on a ridiculous, short-lived, campy *Star Trek* spoof that managed to make it on the air for a full season at some point in our sordid TV history. God bless the exec responsible for *that* decision.

I know that sort of faux pas likely occurs on a daily basis in Hollywood, but can we pause for a moment to appreciate the sheer magic of her mistaking an actress from a top-ten show on NBC for someone who had one line on a show called *Homeboys in Outer Space*? It seriously rocked my warped little martini-filled world.

CUT TO . . .

That warped little world nearly exploded when I had kids. I suddenly discovered just how socially overwhelmed (and possibly inept) I was about to become! It almost makes me feel bad about laughing at that poor, naive actress who struggled with a case of mistaken identity so many years ago. Almost.

MY CRADLE CHRONICLES

According to Wikipedia, *Social Studies* is "The integrated study of the social sciences and humanities to promote civic competence." How delightful! Trouble is, your toddler's sudden interest in the social scene won't promote *your* civic competence . . . or any competence at all, for that matter.

One day you'll wake up to find you've become a cross between a chauffeur and Julie Cruise Director. There will be an onslaught of hectic, overly recreational, kid-centric days that leave you little time to sit down, consume a croissant at warp speed, or bid your husband a "Wassup?" in passing. In other words, you *might* have time for sex by the year 2080. And by then, who knows if you'll still want it? Toddlers are the cold shower of parenting.

You used to pencil in date nights, schedule leisurely weekend travel excursions to the beach, and host '70s-themed cocktail parties with your BFFs complete with a disco ball, psychedelic laser light show, and the complete works of Donna Summer. Now you find yourself planning park playdates, attending princess tea parties, and hauling kids to ballet, tae kwon do, and every other extracurricular activity you can think of to entertain your youngster and cut down on the rampant restlessness. The catch? *None* of those activities include alcohol! (Which, by the way, merely suggests you need to be more creative.)

Welcome to the Entertainment Industry

Here's a look at how your social calendar can become more crowded than Times Square on New Year's Eve. This also may or may not be a chapter about what happens when your two-year-old becomes more technologically advanced with an iPhone, iPad, Blackberry, tablet, Kindle, every-electronic-communication-device-you-can-think-of (she types as she asks her daughter to sign out of the App store . . . again).

The "dating" game.

When your child reaches toddlerhood, you'll turn into such an overworked insta-chaperone that you'll feel like your kid is a contestant on *The Bachelor*. You'll half expect Chris Harrison to peek out from behind the seesaw and say, "This is the final rose" or "Can we get some Kleenex for the girl who just got dumped in the bouncy castle by the little lad in the OshKosh dungarees?"

If you're lucky, you'll find a fellow mom who's fun to hang out with so it isn't just about the kids. For example, the following occurred in our day care parking lot when Gray was two years old.

Me: "We should get Gray and Henry together for a park date or something."

Henry's mom: "Yes! Let's do it! Henry just needs a little notice so he can shave and put on some cologne."

Me: "Fair enough. I think Gray mentioned something about a pedicure and a new pair of stilettos."

Henry's mom: "Maybe we should wait until next weekend, so they have enough time for their date prep."

Me: "Done. I hope he's planning on bringing flowers; she's a little high maintenance."

Henry's mom: "Aren't they all?"

But seriously, you think you have a decade or two to go before your husband is propped against the front door with a shotgun, perfecting his death stare? It'll be here in no time. One day our kids are fighting over swings, and the next we're stealthily ducking behind cars at the drive-in, hoping like hell our daughter isn't smooching a quarterback in the backseat of his Mustang. At least we moms can enjoy one another's company throughout the mayhem.

Curiosity killed the cooties.

I remember the first time I decided to kiss a boy. His name was Bradley (not the same Brad I married, though that would be some epic relationship history), and we were five.

Bradley and I attended kindergarten together. He came over to my house for a visit, and we were in my room coloring. I'm pretty sure I caught him unawares when I planted one on him Britney-Madonna style. Mind you, the kiss was slightly less newsworthy, given it didn't happen in front of an award show audience. And it wasn't televised. Okay, maybe it wasn't the same at all. Either way, I'm sure you get what I'm driving at.

Apparently, even at five, I was a mover and a shaker. I suppose that's not terribly shocking when you consider I also took the initiative to ask my husband out on our first real date nearly thirty years later, but you can consult the final chapter for more on that. Let's just say I've always been a woman who knows what she wants. If it's all the same to you, we'll go with that excuse and pray my daughters are more like their dad, who was a little slower in the "making advances" department. Which I'm sure he's thrilled I've just documented for the whole world to see.

Cooties no longer appear to have much standing in our culture. I easily recall the days when girls and boys screamed and ran from one another like they were fleeing the Keystone Cops during a cocaine bust. Nowadays, kids seem to be desensitized by everything. I've seen middle school relationships that lasted longer than some Hollywood marriages, though I guess that's not hard. Either way, be wary of your child receiving—or doling out—overzealous intimacy during toddlerhood. You might need to have a fun little come-to-Jesus about social boundaries long before you were expecting to.

Once, when Gray was three, we took her to our friends' house. Their son, who was a year older, wouldn't stop cornering her. He was hell-bent on engaging my daughter in a lip-lock. My husband and I kept close tabs on the situation, trying to assess the most appropriate time to step in.

Brad and I didn't want to embarrass the boy or his parents, nor did we want to make a mountain out of a molehill. But as the night progressed, so did the boy's advances. My daughter's giggling turned into panic when he started wrestling her to the floor. I casually removed her from the situation and had a talk I'd never dreamed of having with my three-year-old.

I pulled her aside and said, "It's okay to say *no* when you're uncomfortable. There's nothing wrong with that."

"But I don't want to hurt his feelings," she told me sadly.

I chose my words carefully. "I know we've talked about not purposely hurting our friends' feelings," I said, "and that's definitely important. But standing up for yourself and respecting yourself is even *more* important. Part of being a good friend is being honest and teaching your friends how to respect you too. Your lips are yours to kiss with. You don't have to kiss anyone you don't want to."

She mulled this over for a minute then said, "I don't want to kiss him, Mommy. I just want to kiss you and Daddy and Marlowe."

My heart exploded into a million tiny pieces as my uterus began to glow like it was radioactive. Comments like that make me seriously consider more babies. Shh. Don't tell my husband.

It's fairly easy to see how three- and four-year-olds might get caught in the "overzealous intimacy" crosshairs, but even younger toddlers are vulnerable. In the course of Marlowe's first year at day care she was kissed, hugged, bitten, and squeezed tighter than a rodent before it's consumed by a boa constrictor.

To be fair, my daughter wasn't entirely innocent in the whole deal. One day they caught her sitting on a boy's lap. Another time they found her rubbing someone's back. What can I say? She's a lover. Well, except for the time one of the kids bit her. Then, apparently, she dispensed some immediate karma and slapped him. Oops. And *you go, girl!*

Fortune cookie says the teenage years are going to be a bitch.

Gray decides making friends is a priority on her bucket list.
Photo courtesy of Jenna von Oy.

Amazing social grace. Or not.

As I mentioned in my first book, social graces aren't built in. Our kids learn from observing us, their friends, their teachers, and even the mailman. In other words, you'd better hope that dude's not out there scratching an itchy crotch while delivering your electric bill.

There will be moments you can't help but laugh through, because you have no earthly idea what'll come out of your child's mouth next. Especially during the knock-knock joke and rhyming phases.

Gray once publicly announced, "Hey, Mommy, isn't it so cool that *wrapper* and *crapper* rhyme?" Yes, almost as cool as you saying the word *crapper* in front of a group of people who once respected me. *I love rhyme time. Yes, I do. Complete with public humiliation too.* I pity Dr. Seuss's mom.

There are certainly occasions when I wish my daughters were slightly less brazen about their bowel movements and bodily functions, but I realize they'll eventually simmer down. At some point they'll discover no one is interested in a detailed description but their dad and me. And even then . . . I could stand to go without the play-by-play. Parent or not, *no one* likes to hear the phrase, "Hey, I forgot I ate corn last night." Gross.

Thankfully, kids quickly catch on to the common courtesy basics, as long as we set good examples. Nothing will make you prouder than a teacher or fellow parent telling you how well behaved and considerate your kids are. It's like winning the Stanley Cup of parenting. It also makes you realize your kids are *far* better at remembering their manners when they aren't at home, but every now and again your kid will surprise you.

Once, when Gray was two, a funny little mix-up occurred as I was making her lunch. "Would you like a turkey sandwich?" I asked her.

"Yes, please, Mommy," she responded. "With gray pecans and Band-Aids." A moment transpired while I worried my daughter might be suffering from Pica Syndrome, the disorder in which people consume nonfood items such as dirt and couch stuffing. I then attempted to translate her Toddler-ese into something resembling a sensible meal request. Finally, the light bulb went off.

"No problem," I told her, "One turkey sandwich with Grey Poupon and mayonnaise coming right up. Especially since you asked so nicely."

I can't believe I actually deciphered that. But more importantly, she said *please*! I was very impressed with my polite little pipsqueak, scrambled vocabulary and all.

Social influence vs. social influenza.

When your toddler develops a higher standing in the social scene, the spread of germs is a foregone conclusion. If you're a hypochondriac, you'd better start constructing your designer bubble now. The more your child requests playdates, the more kids he's in contact with. And the more kids he's in contact with, the more hand sanitizer you're going to need to keep in your pocketbook. But isn't it worth it to see your child developing a connection with his peers? Germ-infested gunk and all?

In a manner of speaking and speaking of manners.

Valuable social lessons are lurking around every corner. Take, for instance, the time I was getting Gray ready for a friend's birthday party. As I was pulling a dress over her head she inquired, "Are we going to a party, Mommy?"

"Yes," I told her, "we're going to a birthday barbecue."

"Don't worry," she said. "I'm not going to cry, Mommy."

"Oh, good," I answered. "I'm so glad to hear that."

Then she promptly followed it up with, "I'm not going to pick my nose either."

Needless to say, I was even happier to hear *that*.

Instilling manners is an essential part of toddler parenting. You don't need me to tell you the who, what, when, where, and how of being polite, but apparently some manners aren't as obvious—for children and parents alike.

There are plenty of discourteous parenting practices out there, and each of us is capable of being the guilty party. I'd like to think this occurs by accident more often than not. However, I've stumbled across a few seriously bold offenders. For example, one is a bold offender if one's son drags my daughter off the tire swing by her hair, and one's response is to joke around with an offhand comment such as, "Boys will be boys, huh?" Don't. Just don't. I don't care if you're funnier than Amy Schumer—I'm probably not going to be in the mood to laugh while your kid clutches a fistful of my kid's curls.

In that sort of scenario, justifications generally fall short. Explaining that your kid didn't take a long enough nap won't make up for the fact he just clubbed some poor, unassuming tot over the head like a caveman.

Your parenting peers have heard every excuse before. Most of us have been there, done that, and unsuccessfully tested out the same defense on another parent once or twice. If my kid is being mistreated, I'm not looking for a cover story; I'm looking for genuine compassion. I promise not to react so dramatically it feels like I'm starring in a high school production of *Les Mis*, or encourage my kid to bitch slap yours in return, if you promise to make me feel like you legitimately care about my child's well-being. It probably won't keep my kid from crying, but it'll help my mama bear instincts growl instead of roar.

Honestly, if you can offer the situation half as much attention as the mom across the park is giving her iPhone, that'll do.

Talk-blocking.

When given a chance to handle things on their own, I've found my kids are pretty darn good at resolving disputes with their friends. Parental interference often gives a testy situation more attention than it deserves and makes the parent an unwitting ally. (Either this is true or I'm doing one helluva job BSing my way out of kid drama. Go, me!)

Toddlers have their own language adults don't always comprehend. Or want to. It's a mix of unexpected outbursts, theatrical hand gestures, and occasional grown-up thoughts and ideas hidden behind made-up words. Oh, and it's usually accompanied by a whole lot of pouting. No one can better translate that madness than a fellow toddler. My daughter can interpret a classmate's mood swing like it's Pig Latin.

Unless you feel your child is in danger, or a situation is escalating to the point of destruction, I recommend adopting the role of observer rather than mediator. Learning to resolve issues independently is an important facet of childhood growth. In a world where bullying is a prominent (albeit scary and sad) fixture in our society, your kid is being introduced to the notion of standing up for herself and productively working through problems. Not to mention, how will she become president of the United States one day if she can't even get beyond a sandbox squabble?

You'll embarrass your kids twice as much as they embarrass you.

Right now you're shaking your head and trying to convince yourself I'm full of crap because your kids are too young to even know what the word *embarrassed* means. Well, you're wrong.

If you want to keep on believing in your own supercool awesomeness, more power to you. But just because you fancy yourself a kick-butt, bomb-diggity, amazeballs (and all those other stupid slang words that make me cringe) human, that doesn't mean your child agrees. Even Lenny Kravitz's kids probably think he's uncool from time to time, and I mean . . . come on! Lenny Freaking Kravitz! If you're interested in continuing to convince yourself of your own badassery, my first suggestion is to refrain from singing in your car. Your rock star fantasies will be on hiatus while you're parenting a toddler. When Gray turned two, she became my personal Simon Cowell. My vehicle jam sessions (aka quietly humming along to the radio) were the bane of her existence. She tore apart every note. And apparently, my kid wasn't much of a duet fan. She was under the impression only one of us could sing at a time. Fortunately, by the time she turned four, she stopped caring if we were simultaneously crooning at the top of our lungs. *Un*fortunately, it was Marlowe's turn to cover her ears and shut down my efforts. At least the shower loofah still appreciates my serenading.

Know thy selfie.

Once your toddler knows your entry pass codes, it's all downhill from there. If you don't want your four-year-old to lock you out of your iPad, take five hundred selfies of her big toe, change your cell phone ringtone to a Katy Perry song, or convince Siri she should take commands only from Cookie Monster, you need to have some loose knowledge of how to navigate your electronics. Basically, if you're still asking, "Where's the *on* button for this thing?" you may want to book a training appointment at the Apple store. (If only they offered *How to Beat My Toddler at Her Own Game 101.*)

If you aren't proactive, you'll be learning about photo bursts and the zoom feature from someone who can't yet write her own name and still doesn't understand gum isn't meant to be swallowed. Your iPhone will suddenly start complaining its storage has been exceeded and, lo and behold, you'll discover Barbie games and Strawberry

Shortcake apps abound. Oh, and something called *Sheep Launcher*. Which sounds much worse than it is.

My point? If you know your phone better than your toddler does, you can find more sophisticated ways to lock him out of it. Also, you'll have a better chance of fixing it when he finds a way back in and downloads seven copies of *Angry Birds*. Or worse.

Adventures in babysitting.

Having a repertoire of babysitters in your back pocket is more valuable than the Hope Diamond. A reliable babysitter is your spirit animal. In fact, babysitters made it into this chapter because they're the only way you and your spouse will have a social life (and possibly sex) anytime soon. They are your ultimate saving grace. When someone asks for your favorite sitter's phone number, it'll feel like you're giving away the nuclear launch code. Which means you need to take good care of your sitters so they don't migrate. Here's my mantra: Love your babysitters, feed them, pay them handsomely, and don't ever give out their number to your friends.

Oh, but my eternal thanks to Beth and Brittany, who were dumb enough to turn over their own sitters' contact info to me. I owe you big time! Isn't hypocrisy delightful?

THE MORAL OF MY STORY

As your toddler's social status reaches heightened levels of chaos and happy hustle-bustle, so, too, does yours. Just think—at least you're crawling out from under the rock you've been losing your tan under!

Embrace your growing social calendar. It may not be book club, cocktails with your girlfriends, or catching the new Christian Bale flick with your hubby, but playdates can do wonders for *your* social life too. Sometimes, when the door opens, you just have to jazz-hands your way through it. You know why? Because it means you can *finally* enjoy witty repartee with someone over the age of four who doesn't think fart jokes are the best thing since Wonder Bread. Who cares if your kid spends her time climbing backwards up the park slide or licking sand out of a bucket? You're getting an adult conversation out of the deal. Priorities.

Pausing to feed Gray during a photoshoot, in the final few months of our breastfeeding journey together. *Photo courtesy of Mimosa Arts.*

CHAPTER 2

When Your Breast Friend Moves Away

A SCENIC VIEW OF MY PAST

When I was growing up, I used to pray God would see fit to endow me with larger breasts. I may or may not have done nightly exercises and chanted, "I must, I must, I must increase my bust." I was certain, with enough determination and effort, I would go to bed a Mary Lou Retton and wake up a Dolly Parton. Unfortunately, all I woke up to was continual disappointment and sore pectoral muscles. And perhaps a mild infatuation with gymnastics and sequins. Nonetheless, I didn't stop dreaming I'd eventually look slightly more 3D at some point in my near future. And kids didn't stop making fun of me in the meantime.

We all know middle school can be a brutal place. But relative to the escalated issues kids are facing these days, middle school embarrassment was almost glamorous back in the '80s and '90s. This was especially true in my Norman Rockwell-esque hometown, where there wasn't a heavy influence of big-city, survival-of-the-fittest mentality. Kids had to get creative with their peer pressure, relying on benign name-calling and the ever-popular practice of TPing apple trees in a rival's front yard. When things got really out of hand (or folks were overly bored) a few mailboxes were knocked down with baseball bats, which nearly incited riots at the Town Hall. I think it even made the local paper. That's why, comparatively speaking,

I tend to view my childhood as a tame and civilized time. Granted, there's nothing tame and civilized about the Hammer pants or *Miami Vice* suits my generation so brazenly wore, and we won't even get into crimped hair, mullets, or the perm pandemic. But the issues plaguing me back in the day were small. Almost as small as my microboobies.

One Friday afternoon in the early '90s, while I was on hiatus from filming *Blossom* and in the throes of my desperate desire to fit in with the popular crowd, I was invited to a backyard party at a classmate's house. When my mom dropped me off, after I narrowly escaped her kiss good-bye in front of the cool kids, I adjusted my sexy neon slouch socks and nervously attempted to locate my inner Samantha Micelli. Magazine cutouts of Alyssa Milano adorned every locker back then, so I had some lofty goals.

I made my way over to the driveway, where the guys were shirtless and shooting hoops and the girls were hanging around gossiping and salivating. I blushed profusely when one of the cute boys acknowledged my arrival. He'd already hit puberty enough to shave and wear deodorant, so I was on my way to the big leagues.

For the next ten minutes, I commiserated with him over the pop quiz we'd had in math that day, twirled my hair coyly like I'd seen Molly Ringwald do in *The Breakfast Club*, and giggled as I watched one of the boys flirtatiously begin snapping my girlfriends' bras.

In no time flat (no pun intended), my giggling turned to fear as a premonition of my immediate destiny flashed through my head. What was going to happen when he tried to snap *my* bra? Because, as one might imagine, I had no bra to snap. There was simply no need for it. I mean, what would I have put in there? My homework? Extra hair scrunchies? A poster of Debbie Gibson?

I backed away in horror, furtively glancing toward the woods as I considered hightailing it out of there. But where would I go? And where was the DeLorean when I really needed it? That way I could have transported myself to the lingerie section of our local department store and solved the problem in a nanosecond. Instead, I froze like a Lean Cuisine entrée and winced as the bra-tugging slimeball made his move.

Thump.

There was nothing "snappy" about it. The elastic fabric of my crop top bounced back to my skin with a dull thud as surprise registered on the jokester's face. Predictably, my own face was reddening like a ripe tomato—not that anyone could see it past all my acne.

"Jenna's not wearing a *bra!*" the kid shouted with fascination and delight. Prepubescent boys are merciful like that.

"I . . . I came straight from dance class," I stammered, as if it might explain my inadequacy. But the words fell on deaf ears. By that time most of the other boys had ceased playing basketball and joined in to mock my shameful lack of a brassiere.

And so it happens that, following an excruciatingly long night of melodramatic tears and preteen angst, Saturday saw me perusing the undergarment utopia at Sears for my very first booby buddy.

"How about this one?" my mother asked, pointing to a demure little training bra. I scoffed and held up a more womanly option with red lace and underwire that I clearly had no use for and no business wearing.

"Sure, if that's the one you want." She sighed. (Also known in mom language as *Whatever floats your boat, kid. This is a battle I won't win and don't have the energy to try to.*) Prize in hand, I made a beeline for the checkout counter.

Suddenly, a face materialized in front of me, cutting us off at the pass and nearly making me jump out of my skin.

"I'm *so* excited to meet you!" gushed a giddy boy around my age. His conservative mother was by his side.

"I watch your show all the time. Can I get your autograph?"

(Did I mention *Blossom* had just started making waves and my recognition factor had abruptly graduated from *everyone at our town picnic* to *everyone and his mother?* In this case, quite literally?)

The überfan and his mom stood there expectantly, pen and paper at the ready. I saw Conservative Mom's gaze travel down to the fancy (read: smutty, nearly pornographic) bra in my hand. Mild shock registered as she debated whether or not to shield her son's eyes from the horror. In that moment I went from revered child star to R-rated floozy. To this day, I'm sure the woman blames me for her sweet boy's loss of innocence.

I turned as red as my new bra and awkwardly handed the purchase over to my mom who, God bless her, casually accepted it as if it were her own purchase.

And that's how a young girl's desperation to wear a bra to school turned into the realization that tits are trouble no matter how you spin it.

CUT TO . . .

Several decades of yearning for voluptuous breasts later and what happened? When they finally came in, they were also lactating. *Drat!* And *curses!* Even worse, it meant my new breast friends would be leaving again someday . . . and taking a treasured piece of my heart along with them.

MY CRADLE CHRONICLES

Some moms never breastfeed, some test the waters for a few months, some are in it for the long haul, and some nurse so long they forget what life is like sans self-adhesive breast pads, bras with easy access panels, and a constantly milk-drunk baby barnacle. In case you're wondering, I fell into that last category.

I realize many of you opted to formula-feed, so this chapter may not deeply resonate with you. My intention certainly isn't to alienate anyone, so please feel free to skip this chapter, to read it and laugh along with me anyway, or to use it as a cocktail coaster instead. I'll never know.

The Queen of Wean. Or Not.

My first daughter, Gray, and I were happily attached at the nip until she was nearly two. Since I was already pregnant with my second daughter, Marlowe, and since Gray was only comfort-nursing at that point anyway, we began to wean from one another. It was emotionally draining to say the least. You think giving up sushi and sake during pregnancy made you go through withdrawals? Wait until you give up being a milk dispenser! Despite knowing that it was the right time for both of us to move on, and that I would soon be treasuring a similar bond with my second daughter, it was an incredibly vulnerable time.

The truth is that bidding farewell to breastfeeding isn't just a major transition for our children; it can be challenging for us too. Even the exciting prospect of finally resurrecting your big-girl bras may not overshadow the bittersweet feelings when your breastfeeding experience comes to an end.

I've spoken to women who were thrilled to put some closure on nursing—no more pumping morning, noon, and night or enduring side effects like plugged milk ducts and mastitis, leaking through work shirts, or having their schedules hampered by a need to feed. Not to mention, some women simply aren't super attached to breastfeeding in the first place, which I totally understand and respect. But I adored breastfeeding. I also happen to be what one might casually refer to as a *sentimental fool*, so my experience was a wee bit different. You know, if *a wee bit different* means lactating every time I heard my child cry and openly weeping the first time I saw her drinking from a sippy cup.

To Be a Sap or Not to Be a Sap?

I loved breastfeeding my daughters in a way that exceeded every preconception I'd had, defied a little logic (considering the array of troublesome physical repercussions I had), and frequently defined my early motherhood experience. I loved it through sleepless nights, sore nipples, and being a 24/7 breastaurant. I think it made me a more patient person and a better mom, often forcing me to sit for a few minutes despite the mounds of paperwork, ringing iPhone, and urgent e-mails begging for my attention. It reminded me to pause and appreciate the beautiful details I sometimes forgot to absorb— the sweet grunting noises and sleepy eyes and batting eyelashes, the affectionate gestures like Marlowe rubbing my back and tucking her tiny hands up my shirtsleeves as she suckled, and the way Gray pinched one nipple like she was a lobster in training while simultaneously feeding from the other one. Actually, that last example may not make my top-ten list. Nonetheless, I cherished all our precious moments together and hated to see them go. You may find the same to be true—a postbreastfeeding grief period is perfectly normal!

The last time I nursed Gray, we were skin-to-skin on my bedroom floor. She'd just taken a pretty serious tumble, and we were both in tears. Mind you, she was crying over a bruise on her head; I was crying because I knew it was likely the last time I'd get to nurse her (she types as sniffling ensues and tears pelt her computer keyboard).

At least now you have my answer for the aforementioned *To be a sap or not to be a sap?* question.

Welcome to the Wild, Wild Breast

The notion of leaving breastfeeding behind causes old Boyz II Men ballads to catapult through my brain like I'm breaking up with every college boyfriend I ever had all over again. No, really—"End of the Road," "It's So Hard to Say Good-bye," "Water Runs Dry" (I hope the guys won't mind if I take a little creative license and change that one to "Milk Runs Dry.") Aside from the superspecial, '90s-throwback earworms I've just gifted you, here are a few things to keep in mind as you close the curtain on your epic breastfeeding journey.

All's well that ends well.

The end of breastfeeding may not happen when you're ready for it; it may be dictated for you. In other words, your child may decide he's good and ready to give up the booby buffet while you're still getting misty-eyed over the mere thought of it. Alternately, he may hang on like a persistent case of static cling. You might wake up one morning to find your baby is drinking fewer meals a day or that he just quit cold turkey. The timeline might also be influenced by your work itinerary, a day care schedule, or even medical complications.

If your child makes the decision to move on, it's usually because he's ready . . . even if you aren't. So keep your head up and the Kleenex box handy!

There's a noncompete clause.

American Idol was a contest; the agenda for weaning your child is not. No one is a "better" parent because they breastfed for a longer or shorter period of time than someone else or because they were able to comfortably and successfully wean in three days versus three weeks. Every child responds differently to change. Let's kick those mommy wars in the ass by just saying no to competitive breastfeeding!

There's no overnight bail.

I've known quite a few moms who said, "As soon as my child hits six months old, I'm done with the whole breastfeeding thing." There are no hard and fast rules for weaning, but I'm here to tell you these kinds of things generally progress slowly—whether you want them to or not. Quitting breastfeeding isn't like retiring from a job or giving up chocolate for Lent. You can't resign from it like a term of office or hang it up like a hat—even if it's one of those awesome floppy ones from my *Blossom* days. It takes time, work, diligence, love, patience, and respect for the gradual nature of such a major transition. It can't necessarily be based on a self-imposed set of guidelines or what you've heard is "normal." Instead, it should be based on what you and your child are comfortable with and what makes sense with your lifestyle. Don't be surprised if the process involves some trial, error, and a deluge of late-night crying! Oh, and the baby might cry a little too.

Detachment doesn't have to equal disappointment.

I aspired to follow the American Academy of Pediatrics' recommendation[1] that children should nurse exclusively for the first six months, maintain breastfeeding through year one as they're introduced to solid foods, and then continue for as long as mom and baby deem comfortable. Which means I was setting myself up for disappointment if my own breastfeeding experience didn't quite match up with my grandiose plans.

I spent just shy of two years breastfeeding Gray, so I had similar expectations for Marlowe . . . which wasn't necessarily fair to either of us. At eight months old, Marlowe began cutting down on her breastfed meals. She began showing immense interest in other

---

1 "AAP Reaffirms Breastfeeding Guidelines," *American Academy of Pediatrics*, February 27, 2012, accessed August 1, 2016, http://www.aap.org/en-us/about-the-aap/aap-press-room/pages/AAP-Reaffirms-Breastfeeding-Guidelines.aspx.

foods and getting distracted really easily. Finding lint on the floor suddenly seemed more enticing than partaking in a breastfed meal. This was tough for me to reconcile, because I wanted her to continue nursing as long as possible and it appeared she'd be ready to fully transition to solid foods before I was mentally prepared for her to do so.

My mom had four kids and breastfed all of us, so I phoned her for a little pep talk. I launched into a lengthy diatribe that included a plethora of reasons why I wanted my daughter to continue nursing and ended with a whinier-than-I'd-care-to-admit version of "And I want Marlowe to have all the same health benefits Gray received. I'm worried our bond won't be as strong because she's going to disconnect from me so much earlier."

My mom was quick to remind me every child has different needs. "Marlowe may not feel the need to nurse as long as Gray did," she told me, "but that doesn't mean it's wrong or will affect her negatively." Then, in reference to my siblings and me, she added, "Not one of you weaned at exactly the same age, and none of you seem to have suffered for it."

At that point I considered mentioning the fact that I'm snarky, stubborn as hell, and a little off my rocker, but decided I probably couldn't chalk that up to my childhood nursing habits.

She was right, as moms often are. (But pretty please don't tell her I said that; I'll never live it down.) You know what else? The age my siblings and I weaned also didn't dictate our IQs, career success, bond with my mother, or ability to mature. It didn't stunt anyone's mental growth or set one of us up to be a better future parent. I don't believe one of my girls will be a more stable or loving woman than the other, simply because she chose to exclusively breastfeed for a longer period of time. I also don't believe my friends who formula feed their children will raise less affectionate or intelligent children than I do.

At the end of the day, and much to my selfish relief, Marlowe stuck with breastfeeding for as long as Gray did. But I learned a lesson in all of it. The conversation with my mom made me realize the time we spend breastfeeding our children isn't what ultimately shapes them. The depth of our love has that distinction. It also made me realize that, at the heart of things, my desire to continue breastfeeding Marlowe was as much for my own comfort and fulfillment as it was for hers. I wanted to keep looking forward to our special time together—those exquisite, priceless moments when we were completely mesmerized by one another, learning about each other without words. I wanted to hold onto the beauty of her infancy as long as I could. I wanted her to need me in that way.

My mommy instincts prevailed. When it was time to move on, I tried to set my sentimentality on a shelf and do my best to make my daughter's transition an easy one.

You know, right after I hid in the laundry room and broke down with more pomp and circumstance than at a college graduation.

Bye-bye, Band-Aid

For me, no more breastfeeding meant no more built-in Band-Aid. I suddenly found myself scrambling to find other forms of consolation for my girls when they got a bump on the nose or a scraped knee. In fact, I didn't realize just how much I'd relied on my ability to soothe my girls through nursing. Breast milk was the most powerful tool in my arsenal until it wasn't. But my girls were troopers, and we quickly figured out alternate ways to calm down after tumbles, stumbles, and hurt feelings. That mostly involves the distribution of millions of magic mommy kisses and endless hugs, both which give me the warm fuzzies and make me smile more than that cheeky model in the old Mentos commercials. Ultimately, it's a win-win.

It actually took a while before my boobs—Mork and Mindy— were completely behind-the-scenes players. No, I don't actually refer to my boobs that way. Heaven forbid. But the visual makes me giggle. Or at least say, "Nanoo, nanoo." Let's just say they still had a starring role even after my dinner theatre was closed for renovations.

Until she was nearly three, Gray would slide her hand beneath my shirt whenever she was upset, overtired, or sick. As she put it, "You're warmest under there, Mom." Sometimes she would even lull herself to sleep by softly caressing my chest. Which was lovely and endearing until it wasn't. There were times it felt more akin to Chinese water torture, slowly pushing me toward the brink of madness, as she dug her nails into my chest like a three-toed sloth clinging to the sides of a jungle tree. Still, I won't deny how much I treasured the sacred bond.

An innocent never forgets.

Your kids will eventually move beyond breastfeeding, but they won't forget the impact it had.

One day when Gray was two and a half, we were having a sweet little tête-à-tête. I tapped her chest and said, "Do you know what's in there? Gray's beautiful heart. I have *so* much love for you and that heart of yours; it's very special."

She smiled knowingly and gave my chest a tap in return.

"Yes," I nodded. "Mommy has a heart just like you do. That's *my* heart in there."

She shot me a look of consternation. "And don't forget there's milk."

Mark my words, just because your kid is no longer dining at the breastaurant doesn't mean he isn't still thinking about what's on the menu. He's still having as many dreams about suckling as you're having about making out with Jared Leto, circa *My So-Called Life.* Or is that just me?

Your child also may not refrain from publicly proclaiming his adoration for your breasts, which is pretty adorable as long as you aren't in a room full of strangers. Gray once pointed to my cleavage at a family brunch and loudly announced to our waitress, "Those are my mommy's boobies."

I laughed it off, then avoided direct eye contact as I went back for seconds at the make-your-own-waffles station.

Silly rabbit, tricks are for kids. And so, apparently, are oral fixations.

You may find the end of breastfeeding also marks the end of other preoccupations such as pacifiers or thumb sucking. On the other hand, it may blow them out of proportion like Auto-Tune on a Tim McGraw song. With any luck, your kid won't go from breastfeeding to cramming every object he can get his hands on into his mouth. Because teething already has that covered and then some.

You might notice a different "men"tality.

You know how your husband can't conceive of why you'd want to watch *Pretty Woman* for the seventeenth time or why you insist on deep cleaning the house before your parents come over for dinner? Or how he thinks you're weird for getting excited over an organized Tupperware drawer? You may also discover your husband doesn't understand your reluctance to bid farewell to breastfeeding. You may find his empathy hiding behind that supersized drill bit collection or holed up in the man cave indulging in some foosball therapy. Try to let him off the hook, even though it's easier said than done. He hasn't the first clue what it feels like to lactate (which is probably a good thing), so he has no frame of reference. My suggestion? Phone a friend. It works wonders for the contestants on *Who Wants to Be a Millionaire?* Why not let it do the same for you?

Moving on from the breastauraunt was a tough transition for Gray and me . . . but it also encouraged some beautiful bonding time!
Photo courtesy of Jenna von Oy.

Beauty and the Breast

In general, I've found the mommy community is fairly open about how difficult it can be to get the hang of breastfeeding. When the going gets tough, the tough splash their misadventures across social media and the Internet mommy bloggersphere. Destination: Misery Loves Company. Don't think for a moment I'm pointing fingers—guilty as charged! And I do mean handcuffs-and-orange-jumpsuit guilty. But I think the mommy community tends to be less vocal about how equally painful the letting-go process can be.

Sometimes it seems more socially acceptable to discuss physical pain in lieu of psychological pain, but it's time to increase the awareness. I, for one, am ready to wear my heart on my sleeve and let it all hang out. That is, I'm going to let all my *feelings* hang out, not my ta-tas. I'm keeping it PG these days. Mostly.

Since my goal is to refrain from sugarcoating everything like it's immersed in a colossal vat of maple syrup, I thought I'd spell out some of the possible side effects associated with the end of lactation . . . as they pertain to both the body *and* the brain.

1. Insomnia.

We're not talking a gentle toss-and-turn like kayaks drifting down the Rio Grande. We're talking thrashing and writhing like an earthworm caught in a rain puddle. Have you ever told yourself you could handle a double espresso just before bed, then contemplated giving yourself a lobotomy at four in the morning so you could get a few hours of sleep before work? It's sort of like that.

2. Mammary maladies.

Remember the early days of motherhood when you had to Google every breast-related ailment in existence so you could figure out whether your nipples were suffering from a plugged milk duct or simply rebelling against being a full-time filling station? Well, hang on to your hat—you might find yourself back at square one. Apparently, our breasts are prone to some separation anxiety, and sometimes it comes out in the form of superfun things like mastitis and engorged breasts. You won't be crying over spilled milk, but you might be crying over excess amounts of it.

3. Chemistry experiments.

Just when our bodies have gotten over the drastic maternity and postmaternity upheaval, new hormonal changes go and muck it up more than a muddy English bog. The termination of breastfeeding changes our body chemistry all over again, causing byproducts such as acne, nausea, and headaches. Remember those? They're as dreamy as visiting the men's room at a busy truck stop. Not that I've ever resorted to that, thank God. I'm making an educated guess, and I'm pretty sure I'd like to keep it that way.

4. The return of the monthly visitor.

There seems to be some correlation between breastfeeding and staving off one's menstrual cycle, so the end of one is often the re-introduction of the other. Do you recall the glorious days of cramps and plotting which week of the month you *won't* be wearing your white linen pants to work? How about the sheer thrill of tampons and pads? Well, go unearth your old stash of those suckers, because *they're baaaack!* (Insert harrowing, horror-flick scream here.)

5. You're never fully breast without a smile.

I've heard it isn't uncommon to experience some depression after weaning, due to the shift in hormone levels, mixed with the heartache of leaving that stage of your child's infancy behind. If you're experiencing symptoms of depression, don't be afraid to seek help from your OB-GYN or other trusted medical professional. Postweaning depression is a very real issue, and you aren't alone!

As a side note, I'm clearly not a doctor (unless you count what I've gleaned from watching *Doc McStuffins* with my kids), but my understanding is that gradual weaning can ease the hormonal transition because it allows your system to slowly decrease levels of prolactin and oxytocin. (Whatever the hell *those* are.) So be patient and don't deny yourself the time it takes to work through such an emotional process!

We're Going to . . . Pump You Up

I may be quoting the posing, testosterone-filled girlie men from *SNL*, but I'm actually referring to the can't-imagine-nursing-without-it, saved-my-life-a-million-times breast pump. Because saying good-bye to breastfeeding also means saying good-bye to your dedicated sidekick, in all her dutiful, supportive, steadfast glory. (I'm whistling the theme song to *Friends* right this very moment.)

I have a lot of girlfriends who got attached to their breast pump. And by *attached*, I mean they developed a more serious bond than Bonnie and Clyde. Without the robbery spree.

To those who've never used or needed one, such a close connection with an inanimate object may sound bizarre. But we're not referring to a trivial little nail file or lint brush here. Oh, no. We aren't waxing poetic about pencil sharpeners or toasters or nose hair trimmers. We're talking about the heavyweight superstar of daily breastfeeding assistance and a working mom's closest ally. For the record, I know plenty of stay-at-home moms who are BFFs with their pumps too!

For some women, a breast pump is her intimate companion, devoted confidante, and bosom buddy. You think Tammy Wynette knew how to stand by her man? You ain't seen nothin' until a breast pump stands by her woman! Mine wasn't just my desk paperweight; it was my travel partner and on-set colleague. It allowed me to film scenes while still making sure my daughters were well fed. It also protected my colleagues from wayward milk projections from my otherwise engorged breasts. Which I'm sure was much appreciated by cast and crew alike. In fact, the only thing I've relied on more heavily in this lifetime is my coffeemaker. And maybe my wine opener.

Sometimes parting with your pump can add to the challenge of moving beyond breastfeeding. And because of the quirky phenomenon that renders the majority of us sentimental clutter collectors when we have kids, that pump often winds up in a dark corner of our attic, chillin' with the Christmas ornaments and patiently awaiting its next gig.

Even when there's never going to be a next gig.

So I guess the real question is, *What does one do with a pump once breastfeeding is no longer in the picture?* (Other than sneak off to the attic every now and then for a therapeutic visit, of course.)

A lot of women assume they can pass their old pump along to a friend, but personal pumps aren't technically meant to be shared amongst mothers. From my understanding, there's a risk of cross-contamination, since thoroughly effective sterilization isn't feasible. This apparently remains the case even if you purchase new tubing and bottle supplies.

If you're so inclined, one disposal method I highly recommend is a donation through Medela Recycles. I briefly mentioned this option in my first book, but I think it bears repeating. In 2015, Medela hired me on as their ambassador for this wonderful program, and it really spoke to me. They take our old, used Medela pumps and properly recycle them. In return, they donate new, multi-use hospital-grade pumps to Ronald McDonald House. It's a pretty incredible way to keep our pumps out of the landfills, while simultaneously assisting our fellow moms in need! What better way to end your breastfeeding journey than to help someone else at the start of hers? I encourage you to look into it and consider donating your trusted pump. It's one small way we mommies can reach out to one another and connect on a level we all understand and appreciate.

The Gift That Keeps on Giving

I once read that breastfeeding is so much more than the gift you're giving your children; sometimes it's a gift they're giving you too. I couldn't agree more, and it's why parting is such sweet sorrow for both baby and mommy. Some of my favorite mommy moments have transpired in the quiet calm of nursing my girls, and it's heartbreaking to leave those behind. But that isn't to say there aren't plenty of profound mommy moments ahead too.

The fact is, moving beyond breastfeeding opens the door to other amazing adventures with your child. The structure of your connection changes, but the connection itself doesn't go away. Just think—now you get to enjoy exciting bonding experiences like bedwetting and random tantrums in the toy aisle at Target. Batteries not included. (Please see chapters 4 and 7 for more on those subjects!)

Absence Makes the Breast Grow Fonder

Sometimes it's tough to locate the laughter in the midst of such an emotional and challenging time, so I'm going to do my best to inspire some. Despite all the difficulties associated with the end of breastfeeding, there are some pretty stellar silver linings too!

1. Your tenant's lease is up. Congrats! You finally own your breasts again! That said, your husband might want to move in and get a little piece of that action. Or any action at all, really.

2. You might get some feeling back in your nipples. Twin Peaks: The Revival, coming to a mother near you!

3. You can go back to wearing dry-clean-only shirts. Let your clothes closet rejoice; you're no longer leaking more scandalously than the Pentagon Papers!

4. You no longer have to stuff your lingerie with breast-pad inserts. Which means your bedroom is about to become a more adult-friendly amusement park.

5. You can go to a restaurant, the park, the library, school, or any public place you can think of without exposing yourself to a crowd. Since your kid will no longer be feeling you up, grabbing at your cleavage, or ripping off your hide-a-hooter, it opens up a whole new world of errand running, without your blouse opening up too!

6. Your wine reserve will finally see the light of day. Also, you can go to a wedding reception without pumping and dumping in the public restroom. Did I just hear the heavens open and the angels sing?

7. You'll finally have some freezer room to store that peanut butter triple-fudge ice cream. Your freezer is vaster than outer space now that you're no longer squirreling enough pumped milk to keep an entire population of pygmy goats alive.

8. The size of your boobs might finally even out. Though the jury's still out on this one. My right boob was perpetually in the "always the bridesmaid, never the bride" pickle. Both of my daughters liked the left side better, so the milk on my right side was MIA. Apparently, Lefty was delivering gourmet fare, while Righty was serving a not-so-happy meal. The result? I'm still more asymmetrical than a Picasso painting.

9. You won't secretly think you're losing your marbles when your electric breast pump starts rasping strange messages when no one else is around. It'll no longer whisper creepy sweet nothings in your ear like "Sucker" and "Freak show" while you dispense the goods. Please tell me I'm not alone on this one.

THE MORAL OF MY STORY

The more things change, the more they help you parent. What I finally realized is breastfeeding probably didn't alter my kids as much as it altered *me*.

I don't think my daughters will grow up differently because they were breastfed, but I know I've continued to grow with them differently because of it. Which made our breastfeeding detachment more gut-wrenching than the end of *Titanic*.

Can somebody get me a lifetime supply of waterproof mascara, please?

Gray and Marlowe refuse my help with pulling their preschool backpacks. Par for the course. *Photo courtesy of Jenna von Oy.*

CHAPTER 3

Independence Day Isn't Just a National Holiday

A SCENIC VIEW OF MY PAST

During a stunningly irrational phase of my twenties, I came up with the brilliant idea that I should take a drastic step toward shedding my good-girl image. After years of being labeled the "girl next door" with a "baby face," I was ready to show the world I was a grown-up who possessed maturity and responsibility and all those other fancy-schmancy qualities one typically gains as one ages. Or so I've heard. Instead, and perhaps not surprisingly, my distorted little adolescent mind managed to convince me the most sensible way to prove I was a sophisticated adult was by fast-tracking to Nudieville. Hey, I've never claimed to be the sharpest quill on the cactus.

A midlife crisis can make people do zany things. Some women buy a hot-pink Ferrari, get a boob job, or prance around in skin-tight leopard-print leotards. Or all three, I suppose. Instead, my midlife crisis inspired me to model for a men's magazine spread and play the role of a stripper in a crappy, straight-to-DVD movie. Classy, right?

My parents are very proud.

Right now you're probably wondering how I can possibly refer to those events as a midlife crisis when I was only twenty-five at the time. Would it help if we call it a midcareer crisis instead? Semantics. Either way, it probably sounds more charming if I blame my propensity to flaunt my assets on something other than my own silly, immature whims. And since I'd already been a working actress for twenty years at that stage of my life, I think the midcareer crisis excuse is relatively plausible. Hell, I might even conveniently blame some of my lousy ex-boyfriend choices on that while we're at it. Why not? I might as well milk the fantasy for all it's worth.

To clarify, and this is probably an important distinction, I wasn't actually in the buff in any of the aforementioned magazine and movie appearances, despite how I've made it sound. Was I wearing skimpy underwear and bathing suits? Yes. Was I striking provocative poses and hoping boys would salivate over the images as a result? Sure. I was an insecure, wannabe sex symbol who needed serious validation. Still, I drew the line somewhere before *I see London, I see France, Jenna ain't wearin' any underpants*, if you catch my drift. And I think we can all be thankful for that.

My brief stint as an exhibitionist began with a sexy photo shoot for *King* magazine, which was held at a supersecret location otherwise known as a suite in an opulent Hollywood hotel I won't name, since we weren't technically allowed to be photographing in it.

Champagne was flowing like Niagara Falls, and I was giddy over my scantily clad wardrobe. It had been a while since I'd done a shoot that was elaborate enough to include a hair-and-makeup team and clothing stylist, so I was feeling on top of the world. Or at least buzzed on bubbly and my temporarily boosted ego.

Three hours of hair curling and makeup application later, I was ready to begin our glam session. I was greased up with more baby oil than a 1970s sun worshipper, and I'd donned a racy bra and short shorts that left very little to the imagination . . . except maybe imagining a robe to cover up with.

Just as the photographer began snapping the first few photos, there was a knock at the door. The crew scrambled to cover up lighting equipment, certain a member of the hotel security detail was coming to rain on our (half-naked and somewhat raunchy) parade.

But it wasn't hotel staff; it was Leonardo DiCaprio. Yes, you read that right. Leonardo DiCaprio.

Suddenly flustered, I did what any woman of sound mind would've done. I strolled out in all my hedonistic glory, marched right up to Leo, and asked if he wanted to get in on the action.

I'm totally kidding.

Did I mention I was tipsy and in *lingerie*? I clumsily spilled champagne all over myself, leapt into hiding behind the nearest curtain, hoped like hell the person who answered the door didn't disclose I was in the room, and prayed no one down on Sunset Boulevard could see my pasty white (but professionally oil-slicked) ass mashed up against the third-story window, like a gecko in a reptile terrarium.

It turns out Leo had knocked on the wrong door. He was on his merry way in a matter of seconds, no doubt searching for the room belonging to a Victoria's Secret supermodel. I didn't even have the guts to stick my head out for a cordial hello.

All I left the photo shoot with that day was more hairspray than Mötley Crüe and some obscene photos that are still plastered across the Internet to this day.[2]

My point? We do some pretty dumb things under the guise of "independence" and "self-expression," and sometimes it leaves our insecurities hanging out to dry. And with a lot to explain to our kids someday about why there are risqué pictures of Mommy on the World Wide Web. God help me.

---

2 I realize by virtue of my even mentioning those photos, I risk you Googling them. Which is a lot more attention than they deserve, I promise! That said, I may never get back to that killer twenty-year-old, pre-kid bod, so perhaps I should sit back and enjoy it. Someday when I'm ninety, I'll be flashing those photos to Viagra-popping, argyle-sock-wearing old men during Bingo & Bran Night at the nursing home. After all, what's the point of taking such naughty, indecent photos if you can't flaunt them when your tits are sagging and you're more wrinkled than a raisin? In the meantime, here's hoping my kids never see them.

CUT TO . . .

Watching my kids express their independence leaves me feeling far more naked and vulnerable than any dumb photo shoot I ever did in my twenties. Are you there, sanity? It's me, Jenna.

MY CRADLE CHRONICLES

Independence can be a villainous and vulgar thing. You know how adorable it was when your baby grinned and tested out saying no for the first time? Well, that word experiences a complete makeover during toddlerhood, when it's suddenly used against you all day, every day. And sometimes in the middle of the night too. Any cute factor those two letters possessed when they first entered your little one's vocabulary goes out the window and crashes like a flat-screen TV hurled off a third-story New York apartment balcony.

Know this—as soon as your kid begins coming out of his shell, you'll wish you could shove him right back in again.

Hang on tight. You're about to go tumbling down the rabbit hole.

The Architecture of Awareness

At some point during early toddlerhood, kids begin to notice some basic parameters of the life they lead. They rely on the routines you've put in place and expect their days to maintain a loose sense of structure. They start to develop an awareness of your family dynamic, the rules set out for them in preschool, the nature of their interaction with one another, and the purpose of personal spaces such as their bedroom. They begin to understand the concepts of sharing and privacy and even begin to recognize and put a name to individual needs such as feeling tired or hungry, having to go to the bathroom, or experiencing emotions such as frustration. In other words, they start to grow up (sniff- sniff, sigh).

Here are a few things you have to look forward to as your kid starts to gain some self-confidence and—drumroll, please—form his own opinions. Blasphemy, I tell you!

Next stop, The Comfort Zone!

You're traveling through another dimension, a dimension not only of sight and sound but of mind. A journey into a wondrous land whose boundaries are that of imagination . . .

As your child's independence grows, your homestead will feel smaller and smaller. In fact, it'll feel like you shoved it in an oven and watched it downsize like one of those Smurfette Shrinky-dinks from the '80s (I loved those things!). You may start to think your house isn't big enough to fit the both of you. The residence formerly known as Your Comfort Zone will suddenly convert to The Zone Where Your Kid Expects You to Cater to His Every Whim. If you don't already know, that's essentially the definition of *independence* to a tiny human—*I'm going to sit on my teensy weensy rump, making up a new language with my imaginary friends that sounds eerily like a hamster procreated with Chewbacca, while Mommy cleans up my entire toy collection and fetches me every snack in the refrigerator that doesn't resemble a vegetable.*

As soon as your child realizes he can do things on his own, he'll exercise his savvy new decision-making expertise to ask (demand) that you do it for him instead. When adults do this, we call it *being a lazy, good-for-nothin' loafer*, but you probably shouldn't call your kid that in your out-loud voice.

Toddlers are control freaks. (But not in a good way.)

Toddlers love control more than Janet Jackson. They like to promote themselves to administrative executive and delegate like they're in charge of your 401K. You think I'm kidding? Let the dictatorship commence. By the time it's all said and done, your kid will be designing her own snazzy flag and uniform, commissioning a self-portrait to hang over the fireplace mantle, and taking notes for her autobiographical manifesto. Can you say "Mussolini?"

Toddlers are space invaders.

You know the expression *Mi casa es su casa?* Well, your casa is your toddler's casa and then some. Toddlers are under the impression *everything* in their immediate line of sight belongs to them. This includes, but isn't limited to, your phone, computer, television remote control, and bag of peanut butter cups you thought you'd hidden on a high enough shelf but clearly didn't. You can no longer eat your own ice cream cone (because the flavor you choose *always* tastes better than theirs), and you should expect little fingers to sneak items off your dinner plate every time you look away to pour yourself another glass of wine. So . . . often.

Toddlers stand up for their "civil rights."

Once toddlers establish their own space, they can be partial to the state in which it's kept. In other words, who plays with their toys and reads their books. Or who eats their leftover kettle corn because she got hungry in the middle of the night and thought she could get away with it (so sue me). But do you blame them? I don't like people messing with my shit either.

Once, in an absurd and infuriating debacle we now refer to as The Cat-astrophe, we engaged the services of a new dog-sitter while we traveled to my hometown to have Marlowe baptized. Our usual suspects were all booked, so we took a chance on someone new.

Bad idea. Really bad. Colossal, in fact.

When we left for our beautiful week of family love and spiritual support, I was under the impression I had nothing to fret about. I left explicit instructions (as only a micromanaging fool like me can) and I checked in with our new dog-sitter frequently, inquiring about the well-being of our puppies and asking if she had any questions. Mind you, I wasn't looking for a prize-winning canine nanny here, just a competent one.

By the end of our week away, we were looking forward to getting back home and sleeping in our own beds. After a delayed flight, we got in at nearly midnight to find things amiss. I attempted to put Gray, who'd passed out on the car ride home, into bed in the dark. But when I crossed the threshold of her bedroom, my shoes crunched down on a pebble-like substance. Gray awoke with a start, and I flipped on the light. Fur and pawprints were everywhere. And I do mean *everywhere.* All over the toy chest. In and out of her shoes. On every floor of the dollhouse. It looked like someone had gone postal with a canister of baby powder.

As for what I was stepping on? Kitty litter. Turns out the dog-sitter had brought her two cats over without asking permission. Moreover, she'd decided it was a fine idea to allow them free rein of my child's bedroom! They slept on her comforter, clawed at her pillows, and tracked their litter box contents all over her stuffed animals.

At that late hour, Gray was bawling over the situation. "Mommy, I just don't understand why someone would *do* that to me!" she wailed. "The cats ruined my stuff and hurt my feelings! I just want to sleep in my own bed and I can't now."

I was devastated for her. Needless to say, she spent the night in our bed instead. Oh, and I think this goes without saying, but I put that dog-sitter's phone number through the shredder.

Suffice it to say, toddlers take ownership to heart. Well, except when it comes to who flooded the bathroom or ripped the pop-up book. Then it's always someone else's fault.

R-E-S-P-E-C-T, find out what it means to Mini-Me.

Just because your toddler wants others to respect her personal property doesn't mean *she* knows how to respect it yet. Sometimes kids can get a little destructive while they learn to honor themselves and their belongings.

For example, Gray once came to me saying, "Mommy, I'm sorry I pulled the eye off my stuffed rabbit."

Distraught, she then begged me to fix it. After I explained my abysmal lack of sewing skills (which are almost as crappy as my basketball skills), I asked what made her pull off the eye in the first place. She responded with, "I wanted to break it, but I don't want it to be broken."

Toddler feelings can be very conflicting. For *everyone*. Especially that poor, stuffed bunny.

That sort of internal battle seems to occur frequently in toddlers. It's tough to truly understand consequences without firsthand experience, and toddlers are working to do just that. It's the cause-and-effect, push-and-pull, mental dichotomy of toddlerhood—sometimes they tear something apart so they can figure out the inner workings and put it back together again, and sometimes they tear it apart so they can figure out their *own* inner workings and learn what it means to them. I do my best to encourage my daughters to have respect for themselves, their personal belongings, and the belongings of others. I also do my best to be understanding and emotionally supportive, even when those destructive urges surface. Thankfully, no one's ripping off doll heads or shearing Barbie's hair with a kitchen knife at my house. At least that I know of.

Discretionary Tales.

At some eye-opening juncture in Gray's quest for independence, I realized discretion is something toddlers actually have to be taught. My subtle clue came in the form of my daughter coming home from day care saying, "Mommy, my teachers don't want me to talk about poop or bathroom stuff at school anymore. They don't like it."

"No, I don't imagine they do," I agreed, while making a mental note to make our privacy policy a bit more stringent. And to apologize for her potty mouth at the next parent-teacher conference.

When you consider how much time your tot has spent parading around the house in nary a diaper, sneaking a snack from the milk dispenser by yanking your blouse down in front of God and everyone, going to the bathroom and bathing in your company, and discussing bodily functions for the purposes of knowledge (or sometimes simply for entertainment), it's not hard to imagine why your toddler feels public displays of nudity and indiscretion are the norm. It comes so naturally, at one time I thought my kid might have an illustrious future as mayor of a nudist colony. Someday I'll be sure to secretly add that to her college application.

Having a toddler is a not-so-subtle reminder that discretion is a learned behavior. In other words, if you want your daughter to avoid lifting her skirt to show off those new Minnie Mouse underwear to your bank teller, you should probably encourage your hubby to stop mooning the truckers during family road trips. Kids will eagerly follow our lead, even if we're picking wedgies and eating boogers. We essentially set the tone of tawdry or the precedent of prude. I typically strive for something in between, because I'm a lover of moderation. Except when it comes to consuming Girl Scout cookies. Then all bets are off.

Though it's a humongous responsibility that sometimes comes

back to bite you in the ass, teaching your child the meaning of privacy is a fantastic and important lesson. The truly fun part? As soon as your toddler grasps the concept of privacy, she'll take it upon herself to lock the bathroom door behind her as she heads in to do her business. Then, because toddlers have such impeccable timing, she'll wait until you're in the middle of a bite of burrito before urgently shouting for you to come pick the lock so you can wipe her tushy. Which is *exactly* the extracurricular activity you were hoping for during dinner, I'm sure.

It's a wonderful, impactful world.

You're not the only one who influences your child—so does the world around them. Consequently, where you live can be a huge factor in your toddler's view of acceptable conduct and privacy levels.

Other countries see privacy a bit differently than we do too. We Americans tend to be big on promoting the invasion of personal privacy (think reality TV), while other countries tend to be less prudish about issues such as sexuality and nudity. You can find topless beaches throughout Europe, and women in many parts of the world go braless. Meanwhile, we freak out every time a woman feeds her infant in public, which baffles me to no end. I'll climb off my soapbox now.

My own private . . . anything?

Don't expect your kids to give a damn about *your* privacy, simply because they've taken an interest in their own. When I attempt to go to the bathroom by myself, my children glom on to me faster than belly fat. At the first mention of a phrase like "Mommy needs a little privacy," the popular retort in my house is, "But we *are* giving you privacy, Mommy. We're having a privacy party." It's ridiculous, it's oxymoronic, and it's so dang cute I tend to laugh in spite of myself. I'm a sucker for those adorable little leeches! Even if I can't remember the last time I got to pee without an audience.

In general, kids are wholly uninterested in indulging anything that remotely resembles "mommy me-time," even when it involves the use of toilet paper or shampoo. Why do you think it's so abysmally difficult to find time for sex? When you're the mother of a toddler, your poor vagina is in temporary lockup without bail. Maybe it's nature's way of slowing our roll on the reproduction front, but a shred of alone time with one's spouse would be nice from time to time. (Quickies at 3:00 a.m. with whispered directives and muted moaning, while desperately hoping the kids don't barge in, not withstanding. Don't pretend you don't know what I'm talking about.)

Independence Is an Open Can of Worms

Even though independence can bring out a child's inner fascist, it also brings out their inherent meddlesome busybody. Kids are running, skipping, tantrum-throwing contradictions. Essentially, your child will want to spend half the day being a couch potato and the other half in the relentless pursuit of actively participating in everything you never wanted her to assist you with. Suddenly, she'll have ambitions of being the next Anthony Bourdain, Bob Vila, Cesar Millan, Supernanny, and Mr. Belvedere all rolled into one. This may or may not include wanting to "help" you slow cook a pot roast, build an IKEA dresser, feed the dogs, change your other child's poopy diaper, and dust the furniture. Actually, that last one might be a keeper . . . who doesn't want a little assistance with housework? Warning: once you crack open that door, your toddler will knock it clear off its hinges. The next thing you know, she'll be butter-poaching lobster, swiping the remote control from your channel-surfing husband, and negotiating a pay raise for you when your boss calls.

On second thought, I take it all back. Open the damn door and let that independence in.

Somebody's got his hands in the fickle jar.

Toddlers change their minds like a chameleon changes color. Remember when you had morning sickness during pregnancy? Remember the time you thought you could eat a bowl of chicken noodle soup, but by the time it heated up the thought of it made you want to puke so you set your sights on a peanut butter and jelly sandwich with pickles instead? That's essentially what happens when a toddler makes a decision of any kind. By the time you bring your daughter the red apple slices on the blue plate, she'll argue she wanted green apple slices on an orange plate. When you make peas for dinner, she'll suddenly swear she hates them. When you go back to the drawing board and make broccoli, she'll insist she needed peas because they're her favorite. When you turn on the radio, she'll inevitably cry for the songs from *Aladdin*. When you turn those on, she'll inevitably want the radio, claiming "Mommy, this song makes my head spin." (True story.)

In a nutshell, toddlerhood will make you wonder how you managed to become a full-time maid and butler, right after you wonder if your kid is bipolar.

Who's the Boss?

Part of your toddler's road to independence involves questioning your parenting. Will it be your favorite aspect of this whole ordeal? Thanks for playing; try again.

The first time your child tells you what to wear or what radio station to listen to, it's amusing in an *I like meatloaf but not for every meal* sort of way. You might even indulge him from time to time, but that gets old fast. When he starts picking out new paint colors for the dining room (puke green? really?) and donating your favorite jeans to Goodwill (so what if you haven't been able to squeeze into them for four years?), you'll start to ponder the extent of his dominion. Toddlers can be more influential than Charles Manson. When your kid launches into a running commentary on your parenting methods, the tables have officially turned.

One day my husband asked Marlowe to climb down from our coffee table. When she didn't listen, he repeated himself in a more insistent tone. I happened to walk in at that moment and, not realizing he already had the situation handled, firmly but affectionately told her to get down.

Gray turned to Brad and scolded, "You didn't handle that very well, Daddy. Mommy did a better job. Next time, you should sound less frustrated."

Naturally, she was right, but . . .

In loving memory of a toddler's memory.

You think elephants never forget? Wait until you're dealing with a toddler. As my daughters' independence has matured, so have their memories. At the mere suggestion of a lollipop after school, for instance, they begin counting down the minutes like it's the number of licks to the bottom of that Tootsie Pop. If only we could convince them to be that good at remembering to wash their hands after they poop! A toddler's *acute* memory isn't always a *cute* memory, because their recollection is typically one of convenience.

Toddlers also use their superpowers to conduct mental jujitsu. They're mind warriors of the cunning kind, especially when it comes to dessert and toy acquisition. They'll try anything to get their grubby little hands on a pack of Skittles or a Buzz Lightyear figurine. Take it from me—don't mention anything you don't want to have to follow through on! Unless, of course, you enjoy spending your days being nagged by a half-pint heckler.

A junior negotiator.

Independence hones a toddler's negotiating skills. If I'm ever held hostage during a bank robbery, please don't send in some gruff, Gene Hackman–looking FBI guy with tactical training; send in my kid. She'll talk those perps in circles, lay on a guilt trip thicker than Daniel Radcliffe's eyebrows, and badger them until they hand over not only the hostages but the bags of money too.

You spin me right round, baby, right round.

Sometimes my girls' arguments are so wild and convoluted, I feel like my brain has just crawled out of the washing machine spin cycle. Or, better yet, a Tim Burton film. Other times, I find their arguments so compelling and analytical, I'm left feeling dumber than a bag of Funyuns. There's never a dull moment.

The land before time and patience.

Toddlers have no understanding of concepts such as time and patience. Zero. Zip. Zilch. Nada. Patience sold separately. Here's a typical day in the life of a toddler . . .

Gray: "Mommy, when are my friends coming over to play?"

Me: "Five o'clock."

Gray: "Is that in three minutes?"

Me: "Nope. It's several hours from now."

Gray (precisely two minutes later): "Mommy, is it five o'clock yet?"

Me: "Nope. You have a long way to go, my love."

Gray: "Well, it's too hard to wait, so I'm just going to sing until they get here."

She begins a twenty-minute-long improvised song called "Corn on the Cob Is My Nickname," followed by an equally lengthy tune about dancing purple pears and Duplo trains, set to the tune of "Pop! Goes the Weasel." After that, she moves on to nonstop skipping through the kitchen, while boisterously beating a pot with a wooden spoon. And even though she doesn't comprehend how many hours she has to wait before her friends arrive, I'm *acutely* aware of just how long it will be.

Case clothed.

Nothing reflects a toddler's independence more than his wardrobe. When my girls started exercising some independence, shoes were our first hurdle. By sixteen months, Marlowe had distinct opinions regarding her daily footwear. She would immediately remove an unwanted pair of shoes, return them to her drawer (at least she cleaned up after herself), and hand me a new pair. She couldn't have cared less if the red Mary Janes didn't match the hot-pink romper. Once she had her mind made up, there was no turning back.

It reminds me of the four-year-old neighbor boy who lived across the street when I was growing up in Connecticut—he was obsessed with a pair of canary-yellow galoshes. I never saw the kid without them. It's a 95-degree, scorcher of a summer day? Canary-yellow galoshes. There's two feet of snow and the pond is covered with ice? Canary-yellow galoshes. His mother undoubtedly had visions of Nike high-tops and Buster Brown saddle shoes dancing in her head. A pair of Chuck Taylors probably would've made her downright drunk with enthusiasm. But alas, there were only the canary-yellow galoshes. Those rain boots made that little boy's world go 'round, so his mom eventually stopped fighting it. As I recall, she even let him sleep in those boots every now and then when she was too damned tired to battle it. Oh, yes, did I mention he often paired them with his beloved Batman cape? It was quite the dapper ensemble. He was the best-dressed superhero on the block.

While my kids have never gone to bed in galoshes, I sympathize with the notion that sometimes it's easier to drop an argument and call it a night. As long as your child's apparel of choice doesn't pose a threat to her safety or ability to sleep, what's the difference if you sneak in and remove the cowboy boots later? It could be worse. Someday you'll be fighting over bigger issues, such as whether or not your daughter can wear a miniskirt to school. Or maybe you'll be fighting over whether or not your son can wear one. You just never know.

When the shoe fetish waned, my girls' fashion inclinations leaned more toward anything frilly and sequined. Hats, leg warmers, sunglasses, you name it. They accessorized like '80s Madonna. Material Girls, indeed. At one point or another, they've insisted on wearing ballet slippers to the park, tiaras to the grocery store, and tutus . . . well, any damn time they pleased.

When I attempted to put Gray in jeans for school one day, she melodramatically wailed, "But, Mommy, this isn't pretty. I look like a *boy*!" This was said as if boys were the devil incarnate. (Though, to be fair, I wondered that a time or two before I met my husband too.)

In an attempt to compromise, I started letting her choose one article of clothing per day that I could build an outfit around. That gave her a say in the matter, while still letting me maintain a modicum of control over whether or not she was appropriately dressed for the weather and school. I like that it enforced her independence without letting her opinions get carried away on a flight of fancy. There's plenty of time for that later.

My husband and I want our daughters to have a sense of pride about the clothing they put on their bodies. Moreover, we want them to be proud of—and honor—the bodies beneath that clothing. While encouraging them to make some of their own wardrobe choices may seem like we're instigating a shallow source of pride, we've so far found the opposite to be true. We love that it gives our children the opportunity to be an active part of the daily decision-making process. We feel it lays the groundwork for self-awareness, promotes the idea that their voices and votes not only count but are exeptionally important, and encourages them to be conscious about their bodies and their choices in a positive way. It has inspired important discussions about privacy and appropriate attire, and we truly feel it's empowering them to embrace their own uniqueness.

Then again, it also leads to extra mirror time and longer, pre-outing primp sessions. One night when we were headed out to dinner, Gray asked how long it would be before we left. I told her it would be about forty minutes.

"Oh my gosh! That's not enough time!"

To which I responded, "How long does it take you to get ready? You're only three!"

As your toddler strives for independence, you may find you stop caring if his socks match or if his hair is askew. As long as he isn't wearing a three-day-old, spaghetti-stained T-shirt to school, you might just opt to grin and bear it. Because the fact is, there's something beautiful about watching your child discover his own style and self-confidence via his fashion sense. As long as my kids are bypassing midriff tops, see-through blouses, and short shorts, I'm good with the argyle sweater/sailor-striped skirt combo that makes my daughter look like she's headed for shuffleboard on the starboard deck of the *Queen Mary*. If she's proud of her outfit, so am I.

You know, as long as we don't have to be seen in public together.

Gray exercises her independence at a park playground.
Photo courtesy of Jenna von Oy.

Going stag.

Independence means toddlers start spending time by themselves. *Finally!* (Oh, look! Is that a pig flying? Are icicles forming in hell?) So what if their time is spent littering your kitchen floor with Tupperware containers or learning to pick the lock on your bedroom door? If it offers you five minutes to check Instagram or comb your hair, do you honestly give a crap?

Word up.

I've found independence has bettered the communication I have with my kids. It has also bettered my propensity to lose my patience with them, but I guess that's beside the point.

The more independent my girls have become, the more they're inclined to tell me what's running through their minds at any given moment. Toddlers like to overshare, especially when they're constantly forming newer, better, more stubborn opinions. The sippy cup half-full aspect is you'll no longer be stuck playing charades each time they want something. The half-empty part? Toddlers get a little *too* good at letting you know their needs. Loudly and passionately, and sometimes accompanied by foot stomping.

Speech therapy.

They'll provide the speech; you'll need the therapy. Coffeemakers have a bigger filter than toddlers. They don't like your dance moves? You'll know. They think you look tired? You'll know that too. You forgot to buckle their seat belt before leaving the school parking lot and had to pull over a block away to remedy your momentary brain fart? Not only will *you* know, but so will everyone else. Because it's not punishment enough that you're scared shitless over forgetting to buckle your precious baby's seat belt in the first place; the collateral damage is having to explain yourself to every stranger who crosses your path for the next month. Gee, thanks, kid. However, the side benefit is you'll double- and triple-check all seat belts from that point forward.

Where's the Beefed-up Morale?

Perhaps I should end this thing on a positive note. While your toddler's growing independence will keep you on your toes, it also has its merits. It's the origin of your kid's creativity, friendships, fashion sense, and musical taste. It's also how you'll wind up with hysterical videos of your kid's awesomely ridiculous impromptu dance moves that you may or may not post on YouTube someday. We parents need to amuse ourselves *somehow*!

Most importantly, a toddler's independence makes you realize just how much you're laying the groundwork for the self-esteem and confidence they'll need throughout their lives. And let's not forget, the more you help your child gain his independence, the more you'll get your own back! In time, you may even be able to get through a bathroom trip or an entire cup of coffee without interruption. Baby steps.

THE MORAL OF MY STORY

As a parent, I do my best to take ownership of who I am and what I stand for. The trouble is, sometimes I also want to own who my kids are and what *they* stand for too, and toddlerhood independence rocks that boat like you're on the High Seas. It made me long for the good ol' infant days, when I could pick out cute little outfits that actually matched and weren't overzealously studded with bling, or sing along to the radio without being told to zip it.

Then again, I also yearn for the days when I still had the ass I crammed into that racy photo-shoot ensemble. And I think we all know the chances of *that* happening again in this lifetime.

Gray makes it clear that photoshoots aren't as exciting as they sound.
Photo courtesy of Micah Schweinsberg.

CHAPTER 4

This Is a Test of the Emergency Tantrum-ing System

A SCENIC VIEW OF MY PAST

Years ago, in my midtwenties, I began to spend the bulk of my hiatus weeks from *The Parkers* going back and forth to Nashville to write country music. I was convinced I should be the next Trisha Yearwood or Tanya Tucker, only the thought of cowboy hats and fringe made me throw up a little. Also, I was a Los Angeles transplant by way of Connecticut, so my Yankee-meets-valley-girl accent was a minor stumbling block.

Nevertheless, I was pretty sure I should be able to snap my well-manicured fingers and get signed to Reba's record label. And while I was living in my egomaniacal fantasy world, shouldn't Tim McGraw also leave Faith Hill for me?

A girl can dream.

Anyway, I used to jam-pack my Nashville trips with writing appointments, publisher meetings, and demo sessions. As far as I was concerned, I held Nashville's country music industry in the palm of my hand. Little did I know, pretty soon I'd be holding my front tooth in the palm of my hand as well.

One evening in 2002, I was invited to dinner with a music business friend and several of the Tennessee Titans players. My boyfriend at the time, who happened to live in Nashville, came along for the meet and greet. Would appetizers with football players lead directly to that record deal I wanted? Not likely. But all work and no play made Jenna a dull girl. I mean, did you read the part where I mentioned I would be sitting across from *professional football players*? Guys who make a living beefing up their muscles and wearing tight pants? I rest my case.

We met our Titans buddies at a popular Asian-fusion restaurant near Music Row and ordered a bunch of platters to pass around. The conversation was good; the company was even better . . . Because— and I'm sorry for being repetitive—*football players*. I realize my boyfriend was there, but one can look at the menu even if one doesn't order from it, right? As ogling goes, I was relatively stealthy about it. In fact, I was content to be an unconventionally cute visiting actress, who was fascinated by the current Titans' season. For the moment, we'll ignore the fact that I didn't know a touchdown from a pass.

As I pretended to listen (but actually attempted to guess the girth of arm muscles), I munched on sweet-and-sour orange-peel shrimp. To my surprise, I suddenly bit down on something far too hard to be a crustacean. Just my luck—my front tooth had cracked. And by that I mean that sucker broke in half like a stale gingerbread man. I'm sure there's a country song in there somewhere.

I immediately grabbed my boyfriend and dragged him to the hallway in front of the restrooms.

"My tooth came out!" I told him frantically. He wasn't sure how to respond. After all, we'd been dating only a short time, and who's prepared for randomly aborted dentistry on a fifth date?

"I have porcelain veneers," I explained quickly, shielding my mouth with my hand. "The only way to fix it is to go back to my cosmetic dentist, but my flight home to Los Angeles isn't for another three days!"

To his credit, he handled it like a champ. "Let me see," he instructed calmly. I reluctantly opened my mouth and he surveyed the damage. His sympathetic smile promptly turned into a devilish grin. He stifled laughter, and my face sagged.

"Oh no . . . It's really bad, isn't it?" I moaned.

"Not here in the South," he quickly replied. "Lots of people are missing teeth."

Cold comfort.

"You still look beautiful, even with half a front tooth," he told me. "Now pull yourself together and let's go back to dinner."

"What?" I exclaimed. "Are you nuts? I can't go back to dinner without a tooth. What will the Titans guys think of me?"

"They're football players," he answered. "They've probably had so many concussions they won't even remember it by tomorrow. You, on the other hand, will. Let's get you a drink. After a few stiff ones, you won't care anymore."

He was right. A cocktail or two later, I decided I could grin and bear it. (Without the grinning part, if I could help it.) Once we left the restaurant, I took the edge off my embarrassment with a little trip to the pharmacy for Polident, followed by some mojitos at a nearby bar. I spent the remainder of the evening dancing, living it up, and entertaining my inner redneck. As for the Titans players? They hung out all night, handled my accidental dental faux pas (and drunkenness) with aplomb, and nicknamed me Patty Toothless. Classy? Negative. Classic? Most definitely.

CUT TO . . .

In retrospect, my public dental malfunction in front of a couple of football players wasn't nearly as embarrassing as Janet Jackson's public wardrobe malfunction in front of a nation of Super Bowl fans.

You know what *else* it wasn't nearly as embarrassing as? My kid's first monstrous meltdown in a crowded Starbucks. It's all fun and games until your two-year-old starts knocking over Keurig displays and kicking little old ladies. What's that you say? Starbucks is starting to serve wine and beer in various establishments across the country? Another round for the little old lady with the busted kneecap, Mr. Barista-Bartender, because I'm the proud owner of my very own tantrum-throwing toddler.

Times two.

MY CRADLE CHRONICLES

This is a test. This is only a test. It's just the *longest freaking test of your parenting life*! Tantrums are the notorious thugs of the "terrible twos," but just because you're expecting them to come on like gangbusters doesn't make you any more prepared when they actually do. Hell, you might get through the twos with nary a sniffle, just to have the threes crash in with all the subtlety of a shopping mall flash mob. Which is what happened at our house. It wasn't pretty. In fact, you can just go ahead and disregard all those morons who told you things would get better after the *terrible twos*. Having a *threenager* is way more messed up! No matter what age it explodes in your face like a hand grenade, you'll start to wonder if public meltdowns are some kind of cosmic debt you're paying off for severe social indiscretions you committed in a past life.

Whether your kid throws a solitary tantrum during the course of his toddlerdom (you lucky bastard!) or a number that more closely resembles the population of China, here's my take on what you have to look forward to. Also, how to get through it with some measure of calm and poise . . . Right after you tear your hair out.

The Truth about Tantrums

You can call them temper tantrums, meltdowns of mythic

proportions, hissy fits, conniptions, outbursts, or an attack of the crazies—whatever soothes your soul and/or makes you laugh a little in the face of all that foot-stomping, flailing, and high-pitched shrieking. The fact remains, a tantrum by any other name is still as earsplitting and exasperating.

Here's what I've gleaned from the rather stunning tantrum adventures (especially the public ones) I have under my belt . . .

In the early days of toddlerhood, tantrums most often stem from an inability to properly communicate desires, needs, and emotions. There's nothing worse than feeling misunderstood, especially when you don't have enough words in your vocabulary to explain yourself! It takes a skilled command of the English language to whine, "But Mommy, *why* won't you let me snort Pixy Stix and spend my afternoon wearing underpants on my head, vegging out in a Timothy Leary-esque trance, drooling over brain-anesthetizing episodes of *The Teletubbies?*"

What, you're telling me your two-year-old hasn't requested that a time or five? Give it time.

Once a child hits age three or four, the bulk of freak-outs tend to result from not getting what she wants when she wants it. This may be in the form of candy, a toy, watching addictive electronics, or the desire for your attention . . . Which is the biggie. When kids want a parent's attention, they don't much care if the reaction is a positive or negative one. Who gives a crumb if all the bellowing leads to the loss of a favorite doll, a time-out, or a stern talking to? The fact is, you had to stop what you were doing to handle any or all of those things, and that was your kid's goal to begin with.

Meltdowns mostly result from the fact that toddlers don't yet possess appropriate coping mechanisms for their emotions. Sometimes there's a fine line between overwhelming joy and overwhelming sorrow, especially when you can't define or compartmentalize those feelings just yet. Then again, that trait isn't specific to toddlerhood, is it? I know plenty of adults who haven't yet figured out how to cope with pressure, frustration, or anger. I won't lie—I have my moments too. But as adults, we have a larger variety of stress-relieving remedies at our disposal. We know how to read a novel, hit the gym, book a massage, or hire a babysitter. We're also old enough to purchase liquor. Which definitely works in our favor.

The evolution of a meltdown.

Picture this. You've had a beautifully uneventful morning with your daughter. She woke up happy and carefree, and spent an entire hour playing quietly by herself while you made a dent in the housework. When you asked if she wanted oatmeal for breakfast, she surprised you by answering, "Yes, please, Mommy," then actually proceeded to eat it without all the Goldilocks fussing that it was too hot, too cold, too lumpy, too bland, or in the wrong bowl. When you denied her request for postbreakfast gummy worms, she didn't even flinch. She accepted the pair of pants and sweatshirt you pulled from her closet with a smile and the comment, "That's such a pretty outfit!" And when you said it was too chilly to go outside and swing, she busied herself with a coloring book instead.

What parallel universe are we living in today? you wonder with excitement. Even your internal critic is getting ready to pat you on the back. You congratulate yourself with a *See? I've got this parenting thing down!* And you should! After all, you've managed to dodge the usual morning hysterics like a champ. Initiate phase two of your supremely awesome day.

Hoodwinked by your daughter's easygoing nature, you convince yourself to take that trip to Target you've been putting off for weeks. You've been dreading dragging your kid to a crowded store to shop for Christmas presents, but it has to be done before you resort to stuffing stockings with stale Fruit Loops, paper clips, cotton balls, and miscellaneous art supplies you've been saving for a rainy day. Today the excursion seems doable. Hell, your kid is even letting you sing along to Adele on your way across town instead of suffering through endless repeats of "The Wheels on the Bus." She deserves to be rewarded for her good behavior, so you might even let her get a little treat while you're there. It's a win-win!

But no good deed goes unpunished. Leaving the comfort of your home and entering a public arena is like firing a starting pistol at the Kentucky Derby. The race is on to accomplish everything on your agenda before tempers flare.

Before you know it, you've gone from zero to sixty—a Lamborghini couldn't compete with the abrupt acceleration of your child's emotions. Much to your dismay (with a side of embarrassment), your little angel is suddenly hurling Star Wars figurines and feverishly yanking every Nerf blaster from the shelf.

In an instant that quickly lands a spot on your Top-Ten Most Memorable Parenting Moments of All Time list, someone announces over the loudspeaker, "We need a cleanup crew on aisle seven. Uh, make that aisle eight too. And watch out for flying Matchbox cars; it's a war zone out there."

You grit your teeth behind a smile that belies your desperate desire to hide behind the nearest rack of men's boxers. Your child has turned into a category-five hurricane complete with her own built-in (and boisterous) warning system. And because you've already made the foolish mistake of telling her she could get that damn cake pop (oh, let yourself off the hook—you were outfoxed by the world's tiniest mastermind), you're now stuck multiplying the tantrum by ten when you say, "There will be no cake pop. This behavior won't be tolerated or rewarded."

Cue your child flinging herself to the floor in front of a sign that reads, Keep Calm and Don't Forget to Be Awesome. If only.

May you never have the above experience during your lifetime. May luck shine down upon you like a freaking leprechaun has sprinkled your universe with magical shamrocks. And if you somehow manage to avoid even one temper tantrum during the course of your kid's toddlerhood, please save me a seat at the eternal cool kid's table. Right next to James Spader, if you don't mind. I'm a fan.

'Tis the Season for Some Reason

At some stage of toddlerhood, you'll discover your child's rationalization skills are equivalent to those of a Chia Pet. When you ask him, "What's one plus one?" expect him to answer, "Purple." Welcome to the glamorous life of contradiction and conflict.

Even if your two-year-old has more words in his vocabulary than the Merriam-Webster dictionary, it still doesn't mean he can reason like an adult. Prepare to feel more out of touch than Kanye West as you try to get your kid to communicate with some iota of rationale. The struggle is real. It's best to treat the concept of toddler rationalization like a lottery ticket: pray for a win, but expect a loss.

Meltdowns are usually a response to your screwing up your kid's version of normal. And it's not like toddlers have a lifetime of "normal" to base everything on, so expect the most extreme reaction since North Korea developed nuclear warheads. This is why, for instance, my daughter morphed into a massive anger ball at school one morning over the mere fact that I packed her a blue water thermos instead of a green one. Apparently, there's a life-altering difference.

One can never anticipate what will set a toddler off. One day I saw a little boy at preschool wearing a furry monster hat. It was too adorable to ignore, so I told him, "I love your monster hat! It's awesome!"

"Noooooooo," he wailed, "it's supposed to be scary!"

I mouthed an apology to his mom as she shuffled him in the opposite direction. My bad.

There was also the time Gray awoke to find my husband had already left for work. Since I wasn't her parent of choice that morning, my hugs and affection were turned down like hotel bedsheets. Then the screaming commenced. "Mommy, turn the light off," she yelled at the top of her lungs.

"I can't turn it off," I calmly informed her.

"No, no, no!" she screeched back, reaching a decibel level reserved for cave bats. "You have to turn the lights off. *Right. Now!*"

Did I mention toddlers have only two states of being? One is nonchalant-I'm-channeling-a-teenager-don't-talk-to-me-or-get-near-me-unless-you-have-candy mode. The other is DEFCON-five-state-of-panic-the-sky-is-falling-the-earth-is-opening-in-fissures-of-blistering-hot-lava-so-I-need-you-to-defy-reality mode.

Would you like to know what light my irrational kidzilla wanted me to turn off? The sun.

Now, I may be able to fix a few things here and there with the power of my mind, but convincing the sun not to shine isn't one of them. *Clearly*, that makes me an asshole.

In all seriousness, can we ponder her phenomenal request for a moment? No *sunlight*? For real? Are you hungover, kid? Too many apple juice shooters at snack time yesterday?

For the record, she ultimately apologized by telling me, "I'm sorry I woke up on the wrong side of the bed this morning, Mommy. At least I slept on the right side."

You'll want to combat your toddler's lack of reasoning with some reasoning of your own. Your brain will race to make sense of why your child is acting like a Gremlin who eats after midnight. Because there *must* be some logical explanation, right? You'll entertain the possibilities: Does he need more protein in his diet? More sleep? More hugs? Does he hear the word *yes* too much? How about *no*? A barrage of stray ideas will burst forth like a cannon filled with birthday balloons. You'll try everything you can think of, and then you'll try them again in case it was a fluke thing they so miserably failed the first time.

When you begin to move into the *Why the hell is none of this shit working?* phase (which is just this side of the *I'm about to purposely impale myself with a fork* phase), that's when you'll realize logic doesn't play a starring role in this production. In fact, Logic was replaced by his understudy, Utterly Devoid of Reasoning. Logic was dragged off the stage during the first act with one of those ridiculous canes, and now he's bound and gagged in his dressing room, praying you'll rescue him before curtain call.

Your child doesn't care that you ran out of lemonade. He wants it anyway—two minutes ago. He has zero sympathy for the time you spent making his favorite lasagna from scratch, because he wants a hot dog tonight. You think he needs to take a bath because he's covered in the permanent markers you hid in the very back of the drawer so he wouldn't find them, but he found them anyway? Too bad. What's it to him if he goes to school looking like he lost a fight with Jackson Pollock? Toddlers don't play fair, because they don't have to. Or want to. Or know how to yet.

When your kid dives off the deep end of drama, there's an amusing little retaliatory tool at your disposal, if you're interested. It's a website called assholeparents.com, and it's a tongue-in-cheek way to commiserate with your mommy peers. Parents post candid photos of their kids' temper tantrums, directing blame at themselves, while simultaneously calling out the absurdity of the situation.

The website intro: "Have you ever suggested your child eat a broken granola bar? Have you ever barred your child from playing with power tools? Have you ever served your child a drink from the pink cup when they wanted blue? Then you, too, might be an asshole parent." [3]

Sure, you can gasp and tell yourself, "Oh my gosh, I can't believe parents across the country are putting their kids on display like that! They might be scarred by it later in life!" Or you can indulge your sense of humor, check it out, and have one of the most satisfying laughs you've had in ages. I'll let you decide.

Meltdown Misnomers and Mistakes

There are a lot of common misconceptions regarding toddler temper tantrums. I'm not a doctor, so I can't come at this from a clinical perspective, but firsthand experience is tough to argue. Unless you're between the ages of two and four. Then, apparently, you can find a way to argue anything just short of whether or not the sky is blue. And even then . . . I go back to my daughter's plea for the sun to be turned off.

Here are a few pointers that might help you understand—and survive—the impending chaos.

1. Flare-ups aren't necessarily a reflection of the way you're raising your child. Your parenting methods may not be the cause of sudden surges in your child's emotions—even if it feels that way sometimes.

Thunder is caused by an abrupt increase in atmospheric temperature and air pressure (thank you, Wikipedia), and a toddler's anger is somewhat similar. He's tackling a heightened, confusing emotional spectrum right now! It takes time for kids to explore feelings and learn how to appropriately manage them. That's where all

---

3 *Asshole Parents*, accessed August 1, 2016, http://www.assholeparents.com/.

that kick-ass patience you possess enters the picture. Well, when you can locate it. I don't know about you, but my patience can be damn good at playing hide-and-seek.

2. Your child isn't the only one expressing himself by throwing tantrums. At some frenzied and frustrating moment, you'll wonder if your kid is the only one in the universe who spontaneously turns into the Tasmanian Devil. He's not. Most kids experience an occasional loss of emotional or situational control during the course of their childhood. Wasn't that such a nice and PC way to say *all* kids flip out and act like monsters from time to time? PC or not, you aren't alone, sister!

Some kids experience tantrums more often than others . . . like every day. Some kids are C-4 in elfin human form. While it's infinitely challenging, it's also a normal part of a toddler's learning process. Your little one is gaining control of his feelings and accepting boundaries, and boundaries are good! Even if setting them sometimes threatens to land you in the nuthouse.

3. Tantrums don't usually equate to physical pain. During a child's infancy, parents can often distinguish the difference between cries. One might indicate hunger, while another suggests exhaustion. And there's no mistaking the hurt cry, right? We generally know the sound of our own child's hurt cry so intimately we can zero in on it in a crowd of babies. My point is that newborns don't have the capacity to manufacture emotion. When they're hurt, a tearful reaction is automatic. Toddlers, on the other hand, are becoming increasingly aware of their influence—what elicits attention, what gets them into trouble, and so forth. And this awareness sometimes causes them to embellish a bit. I'll take tantrums for $500, Alex.

Toddlers can be masters of manipulation without intending to be and also sometimes when they *do* intend to be, so don't be surprised if your kid puts on a little show for you from time to time. Why not sit back and enjoy it? It's cheaper than buying a movie ticket, nobody pelts you in the head with Raisinets, and you don't have to sit through thirty minutes of stupid previews first!

On the other hand, you might notice a pattern emerge if you give in to your toddler's theatrics. For example, if your son throws a hissy fit over his "need" for chocolate chip cookies and you give him the treat simply to avoid an ensuing tantrum, you might see the tears vanish like an aircraft in the Bermuda Triangle. Kids quickly discover the squeaky wheel gets the grease . . . and the chocolate chip cookies too! Toddlers have a flair for the melodramatic, and you've got a front row seat. For your sake, I hope the show isn't as long-running as *The Phantom of the Opera*.

4. Try not to be afraid of your kid. No, I don't mean literally afraid—I know he isn't some evil spawn from *Children of the Corn*. But I humbly propose we don't indulge our children for the sake of evading meltdowns.

As parents, we often spend our days dancing on the edge of a razor blade. I just love, for instance, when getting through the baking aisle at Kroger without my kid melting like a snowman feels like my biggest accomplishment of the day. Or like I'm getting away with something. But to avoid everything that might incite a tantrum is to deprive our kids of opportunities for growth and learning. I know, I know. That sounds like some lousy bullshit recommendation that's easy to offer via book pages and not so easy to adhere to. Admittedly, it's a much harder argument when I'm sidestepping projectile Mini-Wheats and fending off two stark raving Mini-Mes! But the reason I even thought to make such a statement in the first place is that I've been at the crossroads more times than I can count.

There are days when *everything* feels like a battle. Consequently, I catch myself treading lightly.

For example, my daughters' emotions tend to peak at bedtime. A long day, even if it's a fun and eventful one, can take its toll. On several occasions, one or the other of my kids has flipped her lid over not being able to wear a certain pair of pajamas to bed. (Toddlers don't care if something is soiled and crumpled at the bottom of the dirty clothes hamper.) And I won't lie, there are nights when I briefly consider fishing out those PJs, smeared with avocado and magic marker, just so my kid can go to bed "happy." And so I can put my aching head on a pillow twenty minutes sooner.

Alas, lines have to be drawn, regardless of how desperately I want to take a free vacation courtesy of Mr. Sandman. Tantrums are like common colds—no matter how painstaking our efforts to avoid them, they usually find a way to sneak in anyway. All I would really be doing is trading in one tantrum for the next. Not to mention, if I tiptoe around impending tantrums, I'm technically allowing my children to make parenting decisions for me. Which means my kids are running the show. And Mama don't play that.

Tantrums can also be a game changer where safety is concerned. One day Gray threw a fit over holding my hand in the day care parking lot. Did I want to cause a scene in front of the staff and parents we've come to know and respect? I wasn't especially keen on the idea, no. But what's the harm in a few curious (or judgmental) gazes, as long as my kid is safe? Let 'em stare, and bring on the hissy fit. That's some entertainment I don't even charge for. Though I might be on to something with that idea, now that I'm thinking about it.

We pick and choose our battles, and sometimes the battle just isn't worth it. But sometimes it is. Don't let tantrums rule the roost!

5. Don't underestimate your child's need to explore his feelings, regardless of personality type. I know a few parents who were shocked by their child's first outburst. One mom I spoke to thought her son was exempt from tantrums altogether, based on his shy and gentle disposition. I thoroughly appreciate how she arrived at that idea, even if it's seriously misdirected.

The thing is, tantrums aren't personality based. Just because your toddler is a quiet observer doesn't mean she isn't working over-time to grow into those giant feelings of hers. Tantrums tend to bring the lion out of the kitten. *I am toddler; hear me roar!* But as we all know, sometimes extremely noisy things come in very small and unassuming packages. Just ask Gilbert Gottfried.

6. Be prepared for some idiot to bestow this lovely little gem on your conscience: "Treasure this time because it goes by fast! Someday you'll wish you could get it all back—even the tantrums."

They're lying through their teeth. Yes, the time goes by faster than a tornado. Yes, you'll wish you could save your favorite moments in a bottle to revisit over and over again. But tantrums won't make your short list. Whoever offers you that twisted "guidance" is clearly lost in a black hole of memories, where logic and truth have gone to die. I don't care how much time passes—no mom enjoys watching her kid pound the wall and holler like a harbor seal. I ask you, what mom wants to hear her child cry over *actual* spilled milk? (For two straight hours, with only a brief intermission to beg for a Kit Kat. And without regard for the fact that a fresh glass of milk was poured five seconds after the spill, and the mess was immediately mopped up. And despite the fact that no one got wet but the dog, who clearly doesn't care, because he's busy licking his balls and drooling all over the coffee table.) Not that I've had that exact experience or anything.

Suffice it to say, I can think of happier ways to spend an af-ternoon than brushing up on my tantrum-tranquilizing skills. Not that I usually have a choice.

7. It's okay to put a little "me" in "meltdown." Go ahead and have a little wine with that whine! No one is saying you have to chug an entire bottle of merlot in order to deal with your kids (then again . . .), but you might want to reserve a spare glass or two for just such an occasion. I mean, why not celebrate *you* in the middle of all that "me, me, me" you keep hearing?

The anti-Christmas card. *Photo courtesy of Mimosa Arts.*

Handle Hysterics with Care

Your reaction plays a starring role in your child's learning process. As I mentioned earlier, your child's emotional outbursts are not caused by some sort of epic parenting failure but rather by the new feelings your child is exploring. I truly believe this to be true. But before you go throwing yourself a party . . .

While a child's lack of emotional maturity might be the direct cause of tantrums, we parents aren't totally exempt. Our ability to handle things calmly and responsibly affects how our children learn to conduct themselves—whether tantrums abound or better decisions are made in the future. It's our job to set boundaries and reinforce them.

While there's no concrete solution for handling your child when he comes unglued, here are a few tactics I've found to be helpful. When they actually work.

1. Speak calmly. According to the powers that be (miscellaneous Internet bloggers and my mother), this is perhaps the most important aspect of dealing with meltdowns. It's a tough one. I'm what I like to call a *passionate responder*—doesn't that put a nice spin on "short-tempered and snarky"? I have to remind myself to pay attention to the tone of my words. I don't enjoy yelling, but I'll admit sometimes the tension and frustration mount, leaving me to a head-on collision with my better judgment. And my tolerance limit. It's easier said than done, but when I shout back at my kids, things invariably escalate. When I really start to get down on myself about it, I try to remember even Gandhi had a few less-than-peaceful moments with his children. Well, I have no way of knowing whether or not that's actually true. Nonetheless, the idea of it makes me feel a little better about myself. Truth is only as good as the mom who can spin it.

2. Refrain from trying to talk to your child while he's freaking out. No one can reason through tears and shouting. Even adults tend to make unreasonable statements and decisions in the throes of anger, so how can we expect our kids to be capable of the emotional restraint we aren't capable of? I definitely support open lines of communication, but you may want to hold off until you aren't talking to a wall. A very cute but very angry wall.

3. Don't laugh. While I generally promote laughter, it's a bad idea when you're trying to maintain appropriate control over your parenting situation. One would assume my longtime career as an actress would give me an advantage in maintaining my poker face, but the only poker face I can do justice to has less to do with parenting and more to do with belting out Lady Gaga's music in the shower. I'm notorious for laughing when I shouldn't. Here's proof:

I took Gray out for an ice cream cone one summer afternoon so we could have some bonding time. In the car on our way home, she asked for a lollipop.

"A lollipop?" I said somewhat incredulously, because I'm always amazed at how comfortable kids are with the notion of subsisting entirely on candy. "You just had ice cream," I told her. "That's enough sugar for the day."

"But I want a lollipop!" she yelled back. (Pout. Sniffle. Wail.) To drive the point home, she followed this up with a lame attempt to kick the back of my seat. However, her legs were too short to reach, which made me laugh. Which made her angrier than a hornet. Which made me laugh even harder. Not my finest moment, but still funny.

4. Once you've set a rule, don't give in! Waffling isn't just for '80s hair and breakfast buffets. Many parents (including yours truly) are notorious for flip-flopping. And I'm not talking about little things like letting your child go down the park slide four more times, rather than the two you originally promised, before you head home. It's your prerogative to give in to that irresistible gap-toothed grin. But there are some rules that aren't meant to be broken, and going back on your own word too often can cause an eventual loss of respect.

When you make a decision, especially important ones regarding the repercussions of misbehaving, stick with it. Stay strong, and may the "reinforce" be with you!

5. Protect your child from potential harm—to himself and others. Kids don't assess their surroundings before pitching a fit. If your little one is in the vicinity of sharp furniture corners, or you think he might lash out against loved ones, such as siblings or family pets, remove him from the area. You may have to drag him out kicking and screaming, but he'll be kicking and screaming his way to safety.

As a side note, courtesy is a truly awesome friend to us all. If your kid starts freaking out and raising her voice while you're in a typically quiet public place such as a restaurant or the library, take her outside until she calms down. We love taking our kids out to eat, and they're well-behaved diners 99 percent of the time. But every now and then one of them gets in a mood, and we wind up leaving with doggie bags. It sucks to walk away from a hot meal, but I'd like to think the good karma comes back tenfold. If nothing else, we avoid dirty looks from the couples smart enough (clearly not us) to hire a sitter for the evening!

6. Sometimes it's OK to ignore your child during a meltdown. As long as you're in the safety of your own home, sometimes it's best to walk away. I'm a fan of this tactic because sometimes tantrum escalation is a direct reflection of how much attention is focused on it. Sometimes *any* response becomes encouragement. This has especially been true for my oldest daughter. My approach is to tell her I love her, that I look forward to discussing things when she's ready to behave appropriately, and that I hope she'll be able to join us again soon. I then leave the room—not to worry, I remain only one room away—while she works through her emotions. This method isn't for every child, but it has served me well with Gray. It gives her space to make thoughtful (and, hopefully, better) decisions and to adjust her attitude.

If you try this method, you might initially experience an internal battle over wanting to comfort your child versus making sure he knows his behavior is unacceptable. It can be a delicate balance. My suggestion is to make sure your child knows he's unconditionally loved, that you're still close by, and that he's welcome back when he has pulled himself together. This way the situation doesn't feel like abandonment, and he understands you're giving him room to take control of his own behavior. Or, you know, to spend the next twenty minutes having muffled, one-sided conversations with himself while drawing imaginary shapes in the air. Whatever helps him sleep at night.

The fact is everyone needs an opportunity to vent. Some people go to the gym, some binge-watch *Game of Thrones*, some raid the refrigerator, and some toss back a dirty martini. Or three. At the end of the day, sometimes our kids just need a bit of freedom to let it all out. So stock up on a few pairs of backup earplugs! (Oh, and I hope this goes without saying, but pretty please don't ignore crying if you think your child might actually be hurt! Safety first!)

7. *Don't forget the best tantrums are the ones that don't happen in the first place.* Employing the art of distraction can be a very useful tool, and one of the most effective distractions is encouraging your child to help out around the house. I'm sure this sounds like I'm having a *One Flew Over the Cuckoo's Nest* kind of moment, but your child actually *wants* to help you. Does he want to wash dishes and clean the baseboards? Not likely. But we all need to feel needed, and assisting with odd jobs around the house can actually be a novel way for him to pass the time. Kids enjoy boredom about as much as they enjoy watching presidential debates, so help them help you! You'll

be amazed at how a lack of monotony leads to a lack of meltdowns.

8. Give your child choices . . . but not too many. I'm a big believer in offering options. When I give my kids the opportunity to make small choices and participate in their own destiny (even if that destiny is whether they'll be having squash or carrots with dinner), they tend to be less upset over decisions they *aren't* allowed to make—such as the dreaded argument over whether or not they have to brush their teeth before school. Or have their hair combed. Or wear clothes.

There's a happy medium somewhere in all of it. Once, when Gray was two, and we were just starting down the rocky road of tantrums, my mom told me I was offering her too many options. As you know, there's a fine line when grandmothers offer advice about how we're raising their grandchildren. Sometimes we want that advice about as much as we want to slam our thumb in a car door or butt-dial our boss from a bar. In this particular instance, however, I was grateful for it. She made me realize I was overburdening my child with choices—choices that were inevitably going to lead to confusion. I'd like to think my intentions were noble; I just wanted to let Gray choose a skirt: pink-and-green flowered, red plaid, blue jean, or purple with ruffles. No big deal, right? But too many choices can backfire.

Such a broad spectrum of choices sent my daughter into a tizzy. The meltdown officially occurred when I nixed the idea of her wearing both the floral *and* plaid skirts, along with the full arm of bangle bracelets she insisted went with them. I just couldn't swallow sending her to day care looking like Cyndi Lauper in training.

9. Don't assume phantom tantrums. This is a phenomenon in which one expects one's child to throw themselves on the floor in a heap of snot and tears at any given moment, only to discover they should've given their child the benefit of the doubt. Oops.

Sometimes our instinct is to expect the worst and hope for the best. That's not a bad plan. But always expecting the worst isn't entirely fair to our kids, and it leaves us in a perpetual state of anxiety over the next big outburst. Live in the moment! And when that moment involves a tantrum, deal with it accordingly. Or hide in a dark corner somewhere with a box of chocolates.

10. Screw the folks who gawk. They've seen a tantrum before, believe me! And if they haven't, they need to get out a little more. Most parents have been in your shoes at one point or another, and most will smile with empathy and commiseration. But every now and then, you'll come across someone who shoots you nasty looks for not being able to "control" your child. This person is clearly leading a quiet, kidless life, replete with the notion babies are robots that heed our every instruction and don't speak unless spoken to. In other words, they're ignorant buffoons. I find smiling and waving is an effective countermeasure.

THE MORAL OF MY STORY

When your child has an all-too-public conniption fit, it's enough to make your hair stand on end. Sometimes you just have to put on a brave face, tuck that kid under your arm like he's a football, and nonchalantly haul him out to the car like it was your plan all along. Is the liquor cabinet calling you home yet?

Marlowe perfects the art of troublemaking.
Photo courtesy of Jenna von Oy.

CHAPTER 5

It's a Hard-Knock Life: A Little Advice on Discipline
(Sort of. Not Really.)

A SCENIC VIEW OF MY PAST

When I was ten, my prized possession was a lavender landline phone (God bless the pre-pager, pre-cell days). It had been at the top of my Christmas list, and I'd begged for it relentlessly. Apparently, Santa took pity on my socially driven little soul and saw fit to buy it for me. Unwrapping that gift made me light up more brightly than the Christmas tree itself.

At ten years old I had no one important to call, and nothing important to discuss even if I did, but I was infatuated with the notion that someday I might. And how could I go wrong with a purple telephone? It matched my very special purple bedroom, which also happened to be subtly adorned with trillions of unicorns and rainbows. If you think *that's* awesome, you should've seen the clothes hanging in my closet. If you were an avid *Blossom* viewer, perhaps you already have.

One balmy summer afternoon, the fate of my phone custody was in peril, though I didn't yet know it. For it was on this day that I decided to take my wardrobe obsession and amateur makeup artistry to a whole new level. I usually just dolled up my little brother, Peter, and turned him into a cross-dressing eight-year-old who looked like he'd taken eye shadow application lessons from Mimi on *The Drew Carey Show*. On this particular morning, however, I took it a step further. Or several steps. I managed to dupe Pete into accompanying me on a costume and cosmetics-clad quest for adventure and excitement. As it turns out, we were also embarking on a quest for a massive chewing out. I've always been a high achiever.

What could I possibly have done with costumes and makeup that was so worthy of punishment, you ask? What's so destructive about satin gloves and sparkly rouge? It all sounds so innocuous! And technically, I suppose it should've been. But I was pretty damn enterprising for a preteen, and I decided to orchestrate my very own clown parade. We weren't allowed to leave our property, so I may or may not have blatantly disregarded the rules when I encouraged Pete to hike down to the main road with me.

Twenty minutes later, my parents were running around the front yard, frantically screaming for their missing children. They checked the normal destinations: our tree house, the creek, and the tent I'd set up in our backyard when I'd briefly run away the week before. We were nowhere to be found. Worried we might have been abducted, they began calling neighbors to see if anyone had spotted us. The search party quickly grew.

Eventually, my parents got in their car and drove around, which is how they finally found us—walking down the busy road in our garish wigs and colorful garb, waving to the cars whizzing by, masquerading as Bozo Junior and Ronald McDonald's kooky and vertically challenged sister.

My two-man parade cost me at least a week's worth of privileges on my precious purple phone, and I haven't been able to listen to "Send in the Clowns" since then. Which may be the only positive side effect of the whole ordeal.

CUT TO . . .

Parenting two toddlers makes me feel like I'm in a clown parade every day of my freaking life, only instead of wearing a bulbous red nose and a plastic, water-shooting flower, I wear my sanity and my heart on my sleeve. Not to mention, the metaphorical shoes I'm filling are *far* bigger and clumsier than the ones from that ridiculous clown getup.

MY CRADLE CHRONICLES

If you're expecting this chapter to be chock-full of guidance on "proper" ways to deal with a rebellious or defiant (aka normal) toddler, prepare to be sorely disappointed; that's not really my area of expertise. Actually, that's *definitely* not my area of expertise. The extent of my good cop/bad cop routine involves owning a police hat and fake badge (don't ask) and watching too many reruns of *NYPD Blue*.

I'd prefer to leave the punitive advice up to people who possess more knowledge than I do (or at least *think* they do), such as Dr. Phil and your mother-in-law. Instead, my goal is to make you laugh in the face of your parenting challenges—namely as they pertain to disciplining your children. Or not disciplining them. Or wanting to discipline them but feeling like society will cast aspersions on your mothering swagger at the mere mention of the term *time-out*.

Reality dictates we parents should be mentally prepared for difficult times every now and then. For the most part, we know what we're in for—kids are going to push the envelope and our buttons from time to time, right? But toddlers don't just push the envelope; they push the whole damn mailbox over. Sometimes steam starts threatening to come out of our ears like we're on an episode of *Looney Toons*, and it takes everything in our power to effectively and appropriately respond to our children without spontaneously combusting. Even though there's no question we love them from the depth of our souls.

When I was growing up, my parents rarely lost their tempers. I recall only a handful of times when voices were raised or serious punishments were doled out. Meanwhile, I feel like I spend every waking minute swimming against the current while wearing cement boots.

Maybe I have a severe patience deficit, or maybe there was simply less pressure for parents in the '80s. Who knows? I suppose it's also possible my memory has built a romantic smokescreen over what actually went down back in the day. That said, I'd seriously love to forget Garbage Pail Kids, Milli Vanilli, and my egregious overuse of Aqua Net, and my mind still hasn't managed to pull that off yet.

Regardless, I won't pretend I don't bite my tongue and force myself to breathe deeply on a daily basis. Life with a toddler can be trying. That's my June Cleaver way of saying it can seriously suck sometimes.

Here are a few tactics my husband and I try to employ (blindly fumble through), when the proverbial shit hits the fan . . . like every other minute. Please note: *Try* is the key word in all of this. The old cliché still stands: *If at first you don't succeed, try and try again.* Then when that doesn't work, curl into the fetal position, suck your thumb, and rock yourself to sleep.

We try to mind meld.

This sounds like some warped, marital ESP thing, but I'm referring to our attempt to be on the same page when it comes to discipline. *Much* easier said than done! In fact, my husband and I not only have trouble being on the same page; we sometimes have trouble being in the same chapter.

My parents used to tell my siblings and I they were a "united front," which I think sounds more like a commercial airline or 1960s peace movement than a synergetic parenting tactic. You're telling me they *always* agreed on how to approach tough situations with four crazy kids running around like Sunday school rejects? That baffles me. It seems so far-fetched, I can sooner envision Mr. Potato Head as a porn star. Not that I want to.

I'm telling you right now, my husband and I aren't always a united front. Unless, of course, *united front* means we simultaneously say the opposite thing, confusing the hell out of our kids and leaving us backpedaling. Still, we do our best to stick together. I hope our kids know that too.

We try to imitate Switzerland.

No, we don't yodel or sing *The Sound of Music* at the top of our lungs during crises. However, the visual of my hubby in lederhosen, blowing an alphorn while riding a mountain goat and shouting "Ricola!" to convince our daughters to stop pulling each other's hair is a keeper. What I'm really saying is, we try to remain neutral— calm, cool, and more collected than Hummel figurines or sports memorabilia. Believe it or not, sometimes we even pull it off!

We try to remember every child responds to discipline differently.

You don't need me to tell you every kid is different. One kid may test the trouble waters, while another dives in deep enough to unearth giant squid or Blackbeard's treasure. Even twins or other siblings who are close in age can have drastically different ways of causing a commotion or reacting to modes of punishment. It's a game changer. Just when you've learned how to expertly reprimand your first child, your second one sends you back to the drawing board.

Our girls have vastly different personalities, so they tend to be motivated by opposite forms of discipline. Gray is a talker. She's an extensive vocabulary-spouting, wise-beyond-her-years, little Miss Chatterbox. (I can't imagine where she got that from.) Marlowe is our physically ambitious child, who was walking by nine months and launching herself off the furniture two weeks later.

Per her affinity for being a motormouth, Gray responds more positively to discussion. She likes to reason through things—even when she's being unreasonable—then sit in solitude to think it over for a while. Once she's ready, she generally returns to apologize. She readily absorbs instructions and files them away for future use, even if she has to be reminded every now and again.

Marlowe, on the other hand, requires immediate redirection, a steady lineup of distractions, and consistently repeated lessons. Don't get me wrong—she's highly intelligent. But she's also a pistol. She's a mischief maker with staunch opinions regarding how her world should be, and she doesn't always care to entertain our rules. She's the reason we have to hide sharp objects and breakable china, lock the toilet seat lid, and post a baby gate around the Christmas tree. As challenging as her antics can be, they also make us adore her even more. Some of my favorite moments have transpired when she has giggled impishly, chosen to ignore me, and continued down her collision course. Apparently, I'm a glutton for punishment.

Some kids are simply destined to blaze the trouble trail. It's a good thing they're so dang lovable!

We try not to resort to kindergarten tactics.

Every now and then I catch myself arguing with Gray like we're conducting a mock trial. One minute I'm telling her to get in the car for dance class, the next I'm heatedly arguing the merits of wearing a seat belt. I've actually given twenty-minute dissertations on asinine things such as why the Easter Bunny doesn't deliver Cadbury eggs in the middle of November.

It's important to remember that sometimes the best course of action is shutting down an argument—firmly, fairly, and finally. Being a parent means you get to decide when to teach a lesson or when to deftly waltz past it like you're Ginger Rogers. It also means you can opt to change the conversation direction whenever you deem necessary. Even if sticking your tongue out and taunting, "Na-na-na-boo-boo!" is a tempting alternative.

We try to offer our kids a friendly parent without offering exclusively a friend.

If all else fails, you've got a friend in Mini-Me. One of my best friends recently told me a cute story. When her youngest son was three, he went through a phase where he would walk up to random strangers and introduce himself by saying, "Hi. I'm Benjamin, and this is my friend, Mommy." Adorable. I mean, who doesn't want their toddler to think they're the bee's knees and shout it from the mountaintops?

Offering a parenting relationship based on trust, love, respect, loyalty, honesty, and an open line of communication is one of the most important gifts we can give our children. That foundation will eventually help them attract friends, confidants, colleagues, and spouses who possess the same attributes. With that in mind, I think it's safe to say we're technically our children's first friends. I love that idea and what it has meant in my rapport with my daughters! I treasure being the first person they've shared secrets and bonded over inside jokes with. I cherish our fort building, silly made-up stories, and kitchen dance parties. Having fun with my girls is, hands down, my favorite pastime. But I also know where the line is drawn. I've witnessed moms blur the lines in order to become the "cool" parent, and that can have some unintended side effects.

Being a parent means we have to set our friendship on the shelf when it's time to lay down the law. Even when it sucks. And it pretty much *always* sucks. When I've had a blissful day of book reading, swing set pushing, doll playing, and giggling, the last thing I want to do is sternly enforce rules that'll spoil our happy mood like the Jolly Green Giant just took a dump on Disneyland. But I'm their mom, and I've gotta do what I've gotta do.

Friends don't let friends forget to put parenting first!

We try to remember kids take things literally.

I once told Gray in passing, "That's the plan, man." Apparently, that particular expression didn't just go over her head; it hurt her feelings.

My daughter was crestfallen. Her face drooped like our basset hound's eyes as she somberly responded, "I'm not a man, Mommy. I'm a girl." It was as if I'd mistaken her for that burly, plaid-wearing lumberjack from the Brawny paper towel ads. Funny though it was, I also felt bad I'd managed to offend her.

You never know how children will perceive figures of speech, and it's good to keep in mind they don't always follow our sense of sarcasm, irony, metaphor, and cliché. They get lost and caught up in literal meanings. Which is an important consideration when, in the throes of discipline, you tell your toddler, "You're barking up the wrong tree," or "Don't count your chickens before they hatch." It's tough to teach a constructive lesson when it's rapidly devolving into an Abbott and Costello "Who's on First?" routine.

We try to maintain consistency.

I know we moms get pissed off when one of our single friends tries to compare crate-training her new cocker spaniel puppy to raising our two-year-old, but putting our parenting pride aside for a moment—isn't it *sort of* similar? The name of the game in guidance, for canine and tiny human alike, is consistency. I'm far from perfect in this department—or any of them, for that matter—but that concept is on my mind a great deal. In part, I suppose, because my own mother keeps jackhammering its importance into my head. I'll give her this: she's consistent about consistently speaking of consistency! Anyway, I agree it's a vital part of disciplining a toddler. And a whopper. Not the Burger King kind.

The more structure and consistency we maintain with the rules we set, the quicker our kids tend to learn and respect them. If they think there's an opening to argue, bamboozle, finagle, or turn tables, they'll take it!

Lord of the Lies

There will come a rather unfortunate moment in your motherhood journey when you'll catch your child in his first distortion of the truth. Chances are, it'll be told with innocence and playful curiosity. And yet, minor or not, you'll smear on the imaginary war paint and prepare to engage in verbal combat. You may get ahead of yourself and wonder if that lie means your kid is a sociopath, bound for a life of posting bail and being on the lam. It doesn't. Nearly all kids try lying on for size during toddlerhood. The trick is making sure it isn't lucrative enough to become the new normal.

I easily recall the first time Gray boldly lied to my face. She was nearly four, and her appreciation for her alone time in the restroom had recently escalated. Not wanting to disrupt her privacy, I'd gotten used to letting her handle her own needs.

One evening, when she exited the lavatory, I asked, "Did you remember to wash your hands?"

"Yes, Mommy," she said.

This surprised me. "Are you sure you remembered?" I questioned casually. "I didn't hear the sink water running."

"You just couldn't hear it because the door was shut," she answered flawlessly and without hesitation.

I felt like I'd been punched in the gut. It was such a small lie in the whole scheme of things, but she'd sold it so *effortlessly*! And the Oscar goes to . . . the almost-four-year-old, post-potty non-hand washer with the winningest damn poker face I've ever seen. Only I didn't consider it a win for *me*. It doesn't bode well for teenage years that might involve questions such as, "Did you sneak out last night to go to a party?" and "Did you run into the neighbor's fence with Daddy's car?" She has a lot of time to perfect her acting chops before then. It's a daunting prospect.

Thankfully, Gray came clean moments later—literally *and* figuratively. I fought the urge to give her a piece of my mind, because I was afraid anger might encourage her reluctance for honesty in the future. Instead, I gently told her I hoped she'd make a different decision about her answer next time, because I would always prefer to hear the truth. (Except in reference to how much weight I've gained since Marlowe was born, but I suppose that's beside the point.)

We went for a long time after that without incident, but that first fib stuck with me. It left me with a deluge of questions such as *What flipped her lying switch?* and *What have I ever done to make her feel a lie is her best response option?* I started over-Googling things (See? You aren't the only one . . .) and found an article that explained: "Toddlers are hardwired to please, so once they see you're unhappy with their behavior, they may attempt to 'undo' their misdeed by denying it. They may also feel they can dodge the consequences that way."[4]

That resonated with me. I occasionally joke about it for the sake of comedy, but *no one* wants to think her kid is manipulative and conniving. Including me. I was relieved to hear that (1) fibbing is very common among toddlers and (2) it wasn't necessarily an intentional deception. "Intentional" in that she did it on purpose, sure, but unintentional in that her goal wasn't to purposely pull the wool over my eyes or break my trust. Her fabrication was to avoid doing something she didn't enjoy—in that case, hand washing. Does that make it right? Certainly not. But it helped my mommy spirit to understand what drove my daughter to do something that, on the

4 "Lying," *What to Expect*, accessed August 1, 2016, http://www.whattoexpect.com/toddler/behavior/lying.aspx.

surface, appeared to be a flagrant act of defiance.

When a toddler tells a tall tale, sometimes it's to evade consequences. Other times, believe it or not, it's actually their interpretation of the truth. Have you ever watched a movie with your best friend or significant other, and you managed to walk away with two totally different versions of what the movie meant? (*Inception*, anyone?) Such is the case with toddler reality versus yours. Even if a scenario seems clear-cut to you, you possess a lifetime of reason, intuition, and bigger-picture understanding on which to base your assessment.

Toddlers have a lot of learning left to do (that's the understatement of the decade), compounded by a proclivity for selectively remembering details. For instance, there's a scenario that often comes up at our house when I ask my girls to clean up a mess they've made. And by *mess*, I mean the zone in question looks like a hotel suite after a visit from the Rolling Stones. Anyway, Gray will often point the finger at her younger sister claiming, "But, Mommy, I didn't take those toys out. Marlowe did." In her mind, the true crime was the removal of said toys from the toy bin. Never mind that she immediately commandeered them from Marlowe, dubbed them hers, and spent the next hour keeping vigil over them like she was patrolling Area 51. A toddler sometimes forgets her own involvement. Kind of like George Clooney wishing he could disavow his role in the Batman franchise.

Even if a lie is whiter than Howdy Doody, it's hard to ignore. Nonetheless, I think the key is positively reinforcing honesty when it makes its illustrious appearance. Which I hope, for your sake, is sometime before your kid turns thirty.

A Bribe Diatribe

There's a myth about bribing, and it goes a little something like this: *Bribing works.* The truth? It can be like making a deal with the devil. I'll admit bribery in its mildest form—as an effective compromise and good behavior reinforcement—can be useful. For example, "If you take a nap now, we can go to the playground when you wake up." No harm, no foul. On the other hand, hard-core bribery works for a short period of time, if ever, and then your kid expects to get Popsicles every single time he refrains from screeching like a wraith through the department store checkout line. That kind of bribery creates monsters, and it will come back to bite you in the ass like a pesky mosquito. I learned that the hard way.

There's definitely a compelling urge to bribe when nothing else is working, but we don't need to teach our kids acting like a hobgoblin is acceptable. Not to mention, it can get expensive to promise toys and goodies every time you want your kid to use his "inside voice," stop bathing in the toilet bowl, or quit pelting the church organist with pretzels.

Side note: If you're gung-ho on bribing, or it manages to sneak its way into your everyday life and wreak havoc like a squirrel in the attic, I recommend avoiding it at all costs during the throes of a tantrum. Bribing midmeltdown is as successful as losing weight by exclusively consuming cake and ice cream.

Anger at a Cellular Level

Moms across the globe might despise me for saying this, but I believe toddler tantrums increase with the frequency of parental cell phone use. Don't get me wrong—I'm guilty of it too. If I can eat lunch, check my e-mail, Facebook a long-lost college friend, and draw a tap-dancing rhinoceros on my daughter's Etch-a-Sketch all at the same time, am I not simply mastering the art of multitasking? While that may be true to some extent, my kids know when my focus is spread too thin. I find the regularity of their meltdowns is directly correlated to how much attention they get from my husband

and me. I'm not suggesting we moms should never divide our time between children and other priorities, such as our workload; that's not terribly realistic. We would have unpaid bills coming out our ears, and the floor would be tough to see past the dog hair and laundry piles. Also, how on earth would we ever find time to post duck-lip selfies and kitten memes on social media?

I'm not passing judgment if you amuse yourself by playing *Words with Friends* while your kid is preoccupied on the park slide, but I believe toddlers are less inclined toward emotional outbursts when we aren't married to our phones. It's tough playing second fiddle to Siri! She's an attention hog, and sometimes she even inserts herself into conversations when you haven't asked her to. If you find your toddler trying to drown her in a watery grave (also known as the potty), it might be time for you and Siri to contemplate a trial separation.

Anger Management

The reality is, figuring out the most appropriate, effective, positive, and successful way to discipline a toddler can wear a parent down. It involves trial, error, and everything in between. And every now and then, despite our vigilant attempts to keep calm, we wind up throwing a tantrum of our own. I have a friend who got so worked up over his kids' antics one day that he kicked a toy and broke his toe in two places! Mind you, two of his three kids are feisty young lads in middle school, so . . . my buddy is in an advanced stage of discipline administration right now, more fondly referred to as hell. Nevertheless, sometimes age is just a number when it comes to acting up. I know some one-year-olds who are very resourceful and creative with troublemaking. Not that I'm calling anyone out. Ahem, *Marlowe.*

Generally speaking, my girls don't drive me to anger so much as they mercilessly try my patience. Toddlers are highly skilled at poking, prodding, pushing, pestering, and provoking. They are also wizards of whining and connoisseurs of clutter and chaos. Have I used enough alliteration to make my point? I've never kicked in a door, punched a wall, or held my breath until my face turned blue, but I won't pretend I always keep my shit together either. Put it this way: If this were *Survivor*, I would've been voted off the island a long time ago.

Parenting is by far the most beautiful and rewarding experience we'll ever have, but it's the hardest one too. Don't feel bad for admitting that! Sometimes it takes a while to see past the irritation and wrap your head around a constructive solution. And sometimes, a *constructive solution* is getting your kids high on cotton candy and Peeps marshmallow candy and then sending them to their grandparents' house for the weekend. I'm just saying.

As parents, we have to acknowledge that home isn't just where the heart is. Sometimes it's where the headache is too. The good news is that your loving mommy instincts will surface even as the warning sirens blare. As long as you keep your anger in check and don't resort to verbal or physical violence, don't feel guilty for letting things get to you every now and then. Walk away for a minute if you need to get your emotions under control, but don't be too hard on yourself. You can't be expected to sweep your own feelings under the carpet. Do they even make carpets big enough for that?

The Good, the Bad, and the Snuggly

As parents, the challenge isn't finding a way to love through our frustration; the unconditional love we possess for our children is never in question. The challenge is making sure our children see that love shining through our words and actions, even when we're at our wits' end. Which can be often.

Sometimes my patience does a high-wire act over the metaphorical Grand Canyon of my moods, and it winds up plunging into the great abyss. But I do my best to live my parenting life as an ambassador of love and affection. Sometimes that love arrives in the form of a hug; other times, in the form of humor. My lifelong mommy goal is to offer a balance of discipline and TLC, laced with a little comedy to take the edge off. I always try to remind my daughters how much I love and cherish them, even when I'm frustrated or disagree with their behavior. The spirit and soul of motherhood isn't just in how we nurture our children; it's in how we handle adversity. Even when that adversity exists within *us*.

Despite putting your best foot forward, your dose of love and comedy may not always work. Sometimes hugging a toddler in the middle of their temper tantrum goes over like a fart in church, and sometimes an attempt at humor makes a toddler dissolve into a puddle of angry tears instead of a fit of laughter. But at least you'll walk away knowing you gave Caring, Warm-hearted, Sense of Humor Mom a shot before Irritable, Needs Some R&R and a Stiff Cosmopolitan Mom excuses herself to go scream into a pillow.

I resist the urge to put my wine in a sippy cup.
Photo courtesy of Jenna von Oy.

Just Another Manic Mom-day

As my friend Beth recently joked, "*In the Weeds*. You should call your next book *In the Weeds*. Because we're going to be in the fucking weeds until we're old." She's right. Sometimes life throws you lemons . . . and they just keep piling up like one big, sour, mushy mess because you have a toddler, so there's no damn time to make something as trivial as lemonade. And even if you did, there's too much sugar in it to let your kid drink it anyway, so why waste the time? It's important to remember *we're* works in progress too. Our kids aren't the only ones with a lot to learn!

Ballerinas are classically trained. Moms and dads aren't. Consequently, we sometimes forget to be awesome. And then we beat ourselves up for it. There are days when I fail to catch my daughter before she falls off the sofa, or I stupidly let my kids extend bedtime by an hour even though I know they're on the brink of a meltdown, or I say yes to that piece of candy even though they didn't eat enough dinner to warrant it. There are times I lose my patience, mention things I wish I could take back, don't follow through when I should, or blame the wrong kid by accident. There are days when I'm too frustrated, too fatigued, too distracted, or too overwhelmed. Like predictive texting, sometimes I say things when I really mean something else. There are moments when I want a vacation, a date night with my husband, endless mai tais being served by a shirtless guy who bears an uncanny resemblance to Ian Somerhalder, and thirty seconds of friggin' peace and quiet. Not necessarily in that order. There are days when I feel like I'm trapped in an episode of *My So-Called Life* instead of *The Wonder Years*, and some days it takes all my energy just to blink. Those are the times when I have to remind myself there's a mommy learning curve no matter what age our children are or what phase they're currently in.

I have two outstanding quotes to throw your way. The first is attributed to Duke Ellington, who wisely and optimistically said, "A problem is a chance for you to do your best." Indeed. And in a perfect world, full of round-the-clock wine bars and babysitters who refuse payment because they love spending time with your kids, we moms would always meet obstacles with unflinching fortitude, steadfast poise, and the patience of Yoda. But alas, we are mere mommy mortals. We sometimes find ourselves mildly annoyed when we trip over scattered puzzle pieces or shoes left in the middle of the hallway. We get exasperated when we're the only ones who clean the house, cook the meals, pick out the clothes, pack the school lunches, and shuttle everyone back and forth for birthday parties and doctor's appointments. But you know what else we do? We rise to the occasion, because everything else is secondary to the love we have for our children.

The second quote comes from (though perhaps by way of some other celebrity, author, parenting guru, or life coach that she heard it from before repeating it to me . . .) Jill Zarin, of *Real Housewives of New York* fame. She and I briefly traded lives for an episode of *Celebrity Wife Swap* back in 2014, and we walked away friends for life. In fact, we may be the only *Wife Swap* participants in history to wind up retaining sound advice *and* a treasured friendship. Either way, Jill gave me some crucial parenting guidance I try to keep in my back pocket. She told me, "You can't take all the credit, and you can't take all the blame."

The fact is, we parent to the best of our ability, and that means something different to each of us. The way I see it, as long as you're offering your child the best you have to give and you're making decisions to positively assist your child's growth and maturity, you're on the right track!

THE MORAL OF MY STORY

Since none of us can completely avoid one or two (or hundreds) of impossibly long and challenge-filled days with our toddler, we have to find discipline methods that keep us from coming unhinged, developing unmanageable nervous tics, and scarring our children for life. Breathe deep, phone a friend, take a brisk walk, or stick your face in a vat of whipped cream (You ask, *Why?* I ask, *Why not?*). Most of all, love your baby through all of the trials and tribulations. Kids can act like shitheads, but at least they're *your* shitheads!

Gray's artistic sensibilities lead her astray . . . or at least into a bath.
Photo courtesy of Jenna von Oy.

CHAPTER 6
Imagination, Creativity, and Other Blasphemy

A SCENIC VIEW OF MY PAST

My best friend Kal and I met in college through a mutual friend. It was one of those love-at-first-sight-but-in-a-strictly-nonromantic-we'd-never-hook-up-in-a-million-years kind of ways. We've been inseparable ever since, though we rarely manage to find ourselves in the same city at the same time anymore. Some folks find it hard to believe we've never been more than platonic amigos, and to the naked eye I suppose we might seem like an unlikely duo. But in my opinion, Batman and Robin didn't necessarily seem like a shoo-in either. I mean, other than the fact that they both wore tights. Is there any better way to bond?

When we met, Kal and I immediately found common ground in our East Coast upbringings and our flair for comedy. On several occasions, the latter has inspired us to take a stab at writing scripts and show treatments together, though we've never actively pursued pitching our collaborations to the studio execs. I'm not sure why that is, exactly, but keep an eye out for us; you never know when we'll take our show on the road. In the meantime, our writing partnership has exposed some . . . ahem . . . rather interesting facets of our friendship. And I wish I meant *exposed* figuratively.

One very hot summer afternoon in 1997, Kal was at my house for a writing session. We were working on a pilot script we were convinced was funny. It wasn't. It was actually pretty abysmal with a bad case of frat house humor. To be fair, we were barely crowding twenty at the time, so our college-attending, adolescent, overcaffeinated, underslept, addled minds just didn't know any better. Or something lame like that. Nonetheless, we were feeling proud of our inaugural sitcom attempt.

We were well into chapter two and on a roll. Kal was sitting at my desk typing dialogue on my laptop, while I reclined on my office sofa in a skimpy halter dress and tossed out cheesy one-liners like I was gearing up for Amateur Night at the Apollo. God bless poor little humor-impaired me.

As I turned to offer up a joke, I glanced at my best friend in my full-length office mirror, simultaneously spotting my own reflection—including Madame Left Boob, who'd evidently decided to deliver her *own* punch line. Kal abruptly looked away and continued tapping at the keyboard.

After a moment of silence I nonchalantly inquired, "Is it my imagination or did you just see my boob?"

"Nope. Not your imagination," he replied dryly. This was quickly followed by, "You might want to put that thing away."

I flushed, tucked my itty-bitty titty back into my dress, and pretended I hadn't just offered my best friend an unsolicited peep show. I should've said, "Don't worry. Objects in the mirror are larger than they appear," but I was finally at a loss for humor. Just when I most needed it. That was probably the subtlest flesh display to ever grace my college experience, which I probably shouldn't admit.

CUT TO . . .

There ain't nothin' subtle about a child's imagination. You can't zip it up, tuck it back in, or stifle it. But why would you want to? *Make-believe* just might be your new love language.

MY CRADLE CHRONICLES

Before having children, I was under the impression that creativity and imagination were going to be the easiest parts of parenting. My whole life has been based on taking creative license with reality, so how hard could it possibly be? Not to mention, I'm secure in the fact that my inner child is alive and well. At this very moment, she's in there sporting a jeweled tiara, clicking the heels of her enchanted ruby slippers, chasing rainbows, and rolling down a sunflower-speckled hill in her puffy tutu. Consequently, indulging my children's imaginations seemed like something I'd have no trouble doing. I was eager to turn moving boxes into pirate ships and cloud castles and a big-top circus tent. I yearned to sail across the ocean blue in a milk carton and fly through the air in a plane made of sofa cushions. I couldn't wait to create a winter wonderland by snipping paper snowflakes or build an undersea utopia simply by scrounging up some cardboard and crayons.

Until I realized just how much freaking *work* it all is. It's a never-ending trip to Neverland! Because kids imagine and invent things every waking moment of every day, without regard for time constraints or your current level of fatigue. They don't care if your in-laws are coming for the weekend and you've *finally* finished deep cleaning the house, or that the soup is going to burn if you don't stir it immediately. They don't care if you're exhausted, PMSing, in the middle of a work deadline, haven't eaten since breakfast, haven't had enough coffee, had too much coffee and really have to pee, or just accidentally stabbed yourself in the eye with a chopstick. And it's not like any of us can get away with hours of tearing things apart and then say to our spouse, "Hey, you're finally home from work. Would you be a dear and clean up the pillow fort village we built? I'm too darn tuckered out from impersonating a four-year-old all day."

Kids' imaginations refuse limitations, which is a blessing and a curse. They don't want one story before bedtime; they want five. And they want you to make one up from scratch because "There are no good books on the shelf, Mommy," even though there are enough to start your own library and charge admission. Oh, and "You'd better not tell the same story you told last night. Tonight I want a reeeeeally long one about fireflies with light switches and a shooting star and a mouse with a polka-dot umbrella."

Apparently, the moment you eject a baby from your vagina, you become an impromptu storytelling genius.

But back to our regularly scheduled programming.

The Evil Spawns of Creation and Imagination

Here are some of the barbaric—um . . . I mean, beautiful— things you have to look forward to as your toddler learns to bulldoze the bounds of fantasy, invention, creativity, and make-believe.

A question-and-answer obsession.

We all know kids have inquiring minds, but toddlers are more fanatical about asking questions than Comic-Con groupies are about cosplay costumes. Expect the twenty-one-question routine from your kid. Unless, God forbid, you have an *exceedingly* curious one like mine—in which case, twenty-one doesn't even come close to covering it. Twenty-one would be a gift.

When Gray turned two, she started coming up with wild queries. And I mean Pythagoras wild—intense brilliance mixed with a metaphysical quality that leaves me totally stumped more often than not. In case you enjoy random factoids as much as I do—you never know when you'll need them for Trivial Pursuit— Pythagoras created the Pythagorean theorem. Purportedly, he also founded a religion based on the notion of demonic beans. Yes, beans. Not the magic kind Jack planted to grow his beanstalk to the giant's kingdom in the clouds; the kind you put in your chili. Or at least that's what I gleaned from Wikipedia. Anyway, the off-the-wall questions began the *very* next day after Gray turned two. It was like she'd been transformed into a pint-sized, instaphilosopher overnight. Once they started, they never stopped. It was as if she'd been putting everything on an internal memory drive that had suddenly finished uploading. And don't think for a second they were simple things like "What color is orange juice?" or "Why do you laugh at your own jokes, Mommy?" One day my kid was making trivial inquiries that made me feel like I was smarter than the average bear, and the next she was hitting me up with things like, "Why do humans live on earth instead of another planet?" and "I know *who* God is, but exactly *what* is God?" Cue my stuttering and mild shock. I began wishing I'd made better friends with Bill Nye the Science Guy years before, when I guested on the first episode of his series. (C'mon, who didn't love hearing Six downing a double espresso and speed-talking through an explanation about the Earth's crust?)

As it turns out, toddler moms should keep a full team of scientists, astrologists, doctors, and religious experts on 24/7 retainer. My daughter's wonderful world of "Why?" had me feeling like a full-time *Jeopardy* contestant. Here's a sampling from Gray's repertoire:

1. "How come people have hair and houses don't?"
2. "Why do we have to wear clothes when we go out for a walk?"
3. "Why do we have skin to cover our bones?"
4. "Why does grass grow outside but not inside?"
5. "Why do people have faces?"
6. "Why can't rain come from the sun?"
7. "How did Marlowe come out of your tummy?"
8. "If Marlowe lived on the inside of your body, and there's

blood in there, did she have your blood on her when she came out?"

9. "When we dream, why do our minds travel someplace else when our bodies don't move?"

10. "Mommy, why can't you answer my questions sometimes?"

Did I mention all of those were asked during the course of a solitary, 10-minute car ride?

I love having inquisitive kids, but here's the rub—as much as I relish the idea of pondering the meaning of life and scientific theory with my daughters over shots of Tang, I actually have to come up with legitimate answers to the questions I'm asked. Answers that satisfy my daughters' curiosity and an appropriate version of the truth, while still making sense to people who haven't yet figured out how to tie their own shoelaces or spit after they gargle. It's easier said than done. Every now and then you might be able to get away with changing the subject or offering a shallow response to deep questions, because you can tell your child stumbled upon them by accident. Other times you'll recognize the intense concentration in her eyes and know there's no escape—whether you're prepared to give a thoughtful answer or not.

Kids have an uncanny ability to make us resurrect every science and history lesson we vaguely paid attention to in grade school. And just as soon as you're feeling pleased that you've managed to answer everything truthfully and age-appropriately, your kid will come up with some mind-blowing question that leaves you befuddled. So, you know, good luck with that.

The creativity might "wear" you out.

If your kids are anything like mine, you'll spend a significant amount of time decked out in random objects you generally reserve for activities such as cooking and sleeping. You'll wind up with dish towel bonnets and bedsheet togas. You might even end up sporting an underwear necklace (I hope, for your sake, the bloomers at least come from the clean laundry pile) and a belt made of lasagna noodles. My former *Blossom* costar, Mayim Bialik, once told me she spent much of her sons' childhood being made to wear bike helmets. My own daughter used to bestow my husband with an ornately embellished tiara during their weekend tea parties. And in answer to your next question—yes, I took pictures. Lots of them. What kind of fool do you take me for?

Your kid will make stuff up that makes no sense.
But not making any sense can be exciting and wonderful too! Even when your toddler's ideas are so warped and psychedelic they totally weird you out and you secretly (or not so secretly) wonder if he's a teensy weensy Timothy Leary wannabe who's managed to score LSD from a local underground day care drug-dealing ring. Okay, now I'm really getting carried away. I hope to God that sort of thing doesn't actually exist! Nevertheless, don't fret over the strange behavior. It simply means your child is exploring the bounds of fantasy and reality and making choices about how he's influenced by them both.

The stories my girls tell are typically a combination of fact and fiction. They also tend to run longer than the *Roots* miniseries, but I'm their mother; storytelling brevity just isn't in the genes. Gray once made up a fable about a bunny rabbit that wanted to eat an orange flower. The bunny's mother told him the flower wasn't edible (yup, my three-year-old actually used the word *edible*), so he ate a sparkly rainbow instead and wound up with a tummy ache. A rabbit eating flowers? Totally feasible. But when the rabbit started munching on sparkly rainbows, I think we crossed into good ol' Fantasyland. Or got beamed into an episode of *H.R. Pufnstuf.*

My point is sometimes your kids will come up with bizarre comments, explanations, or adventurous tales, and it's okay to humor them. You don't have to be their permanent, Debbie Downer reality check. Why put a gag order on imagination? An imagination stifler is a dream squasher.

That reminds me of the time the illusion of Mickey Mouse was crushed for me. I was backstage at Epcot and a guy in costume was smoking a cigarette with one hand while holding his Mickey head in the other. Even a few refrains of "It's a Small World" couldn't bring me back from that visual. *The Magical World of Disney*, indeed.

You aren't alone in the madness.

You may not know what the hell your toddler is talking about half the time. But you know what? Neither does he.

Once, after one of Gray's lengthy, head-spinning narratives that left me feeling like someone slipped me a Mickey (the drink, not the aforementioned mouse), I asked my then-two-year-old daughter, "I don't understand. What are you saying?"

To which she replied, "I don't know, actually. It's a problem."

You see? We parents aren't living alone out there in Crazytown.

Rainy days spell T-R-O-U-B-L-E.

This is an egregious understatement. A toddler plus cabin fever equals a terrible, horrible, no good, very bad day. Or, God help you, week. If you live in Seattle, I hope you have an indoor jungle gym at your disposal, and if you live in the Amazon rainforest, you're way beyond my help. Then again, Tarzan seemed to do just fine, so maybe you're onto something.

Rainy days turn kids into wild savages, made exponentially worse if—in some moment of temporary insanity—you think it's okay to give them sugar. Sugar is your arch nemesis. If you aren't careful, your little one will be worshiping at the altar of candy and cookies and begging to mainline Capri Suns ten minutes before bedtime. Those are the gateway drug. Ladies, lock up your Godivas and gummy bears! You know how they say you shouldn't feed the animals at the zoo? Well, feeding your little one sweets can have an intensely rowdier result. Hyenas have nothing on sugar-buzzed kiddos. Toddlers get loopier than a theme park roller coaster if they even *smell* sugar. In no time flat you'll be trying to lasso a moving, yelling target as he swings from the rafters or rushes your china cabinet like a sumo wrestler. Or worse. As Gray once told me after an ice cream overdose, "Mommy, sugar makes me angry inside." Which was an astute observation for a three-year-old, in my opinion. Not that it stopped her from asking for a piece of pie ten minutes later.

My advice? Save a mason jar filled with fun ideas (the Internet won't disappoint if you need help coming up with some), and retrieve that sucker as soon as the storm clouds start gathering. As a second—but no less effective—option, save a mason jar filled with moonshine instead, and sneak away for a slug when you're just shy of tearing your hair out.

Gray's infamous Thanksgiving turkey handprint . . . which isn't for the faint of heart. *Photo courtesy of Jenna von Oy.*

The Art of War

A few other things to consider in the quest to keep up with your child's newly discovered imagination . . .

It's important to recognize the symptoms of an "art attack."

If you have a budding artist, you'll know it. Let me rephrase that. If you have a budding artist, every room in your *house* will know it. It will be recognizable by the obvious telltale signs—paper doll cutouts in every back issue of *Vogue* you've been saving since you were thirteen, the fact that there are twice as many crayon markings as magnets on your refrigerator, the nightly food collage you have to scrub from your kid's place mat, and the pesky neon Play-Doh embedded in your rugs. I won't even get into what sort of finger painting can be done on the bathroom walls if you aren't careful. Let's just say it's a *crappy* mess to clean up.

You may also find future projects stashed in sock drawers and stowed under the bed. Everything can be a masterpiece when your child is resourceful! I was at a friend's house once, and her son came out to see if we had anything he could use to assemble a mini army of samurai warriors. "Art is kinda like my *thing* now," he announced. We scrounged up a few champagne corks that did the trick. And by that I mean my friend and I drank a few bottles of champagne in the name of helping his artistry along. I know, I know. We're such martyrs.

When Gray was three, she went through a phase during which she stockpiled empty toilet paper rolls and dried leaves. "I'm going to make something with these someday," she informed me . . . Right after she chastised me for throwing out a T-shirt with multiple holes under the armpits that she swore would also come in handy. I guess I can eliminate housekeeping and trash collection from the list of possible career paths for that girl. On the other hand, the jury is still out on fashion design.

In short, you may find your Warhol protégé leaving behind an infinite trail of crafty clutter and mayhem. A true artist, indeed! Now let's just hope when you have to draw the line, your kid doesn't retaliate by drawing a line of his own . . . right down the hall corridor in red Sharpie.

There's no crime like the present.

People (usually extended family) will eagerly praise their own heroism for gifting your children with innovative, mind-expanding toys on birthdays and holidays. This is otherwise known as *Those fools don't have a dog in the hunt, so they can get away with giving your kid whatever they want.* They don't have to buy earplugs when your son forms a one-man band with the five-piece drum set they sent, or launder the sticky, sparkly explosion on your new comforter that resulted from a science experiment kit gone awry. They don't have to pick up the itty-bitty necklace beads that scattered under your coffee table like rat turds or explain why live butterflies have to be released into the wild after they emerge from their happy little in-home habitat cocoons (but I still love you, Alyssa and Tony!). They're perfectly comfortable fostering your child's creativity with grandiose offerings of joy and amusement because they don't have to clean up the mess. There's probably nothing you can say to deter them, so my suggestion? Wait until they have kids of their own and return the favor tenfold, or send your kids *and* those new toys over to their house for a sleepover while you stay home and make a colossal batch of margaritas. Olé!

Don't be afraid to "class" things up.

Kids need to be challenged. Some kids, like Gray, need constant mental stimulation. Others, like my little Marlowe, are in need of endless physical stimulation—her feet never stop moving. And I mean *never.*

The fact is it's tough to be 100 percent responsible for keeping a child busy 100 percent of the time. Yes, you're the mom and, yes, you should have some seriously kick-ass tricks up your sleeve to entertain your kids. Hell, sometimes I'm a one-woman game-inventing, book-reading, potato-juggling, magic-show-hosting puppeteer. But it's also good to let other people give a little assistance in this department, if at all possible. Every now and then you need a lunch break. Or a potty break. Or a sneak-a-Snickers-in-the-closet break.

Sending your kid to an hour of dancing, soccer, music, or tumbling might give your arms a much-needed intermission from pushing him in the swing for ten straight hours.

More often than not, letting your toddler engage in activities outside your everyday arena does a more thorough job of getting restless energy out. My kids have a tendency to be more entertained by everyone else but me because the structure change is novel and exciting.

Preschool is an outstanding source of extracurricular activities. You want a sponsored energy release? Those teachers will watch your kid splash in kiddie pools, sift through sandboxes, and scale the monkey bars like . . . well, a monkey. And the art projects! Oh, the art projects! Schools are ready, able, and willing to deal with a constant mess, and they're prepared for it in much the same way a farmer is prepared to step in pig shit all the live long day. Being your kid's housekeeping shadow probably isn't their favorite part of the gig, but it comes with the territory. Which means they've got a surplus of everything from paper towels and sanitizer to construction paper and colored cotton balls. Pipe cleaners, Popsicle sticks, and glitter, oh my! It's worth sending your kid to day care just so he'll return with exceptionally amusing homemade art. If you win the preschool art lottery, your child will make you a Thanksgiving turkey from her handprint that looks like it has already been slaughtered for the feast. For the record, that's one of my prized possessions from Gray's toddler days, and it's a keeper. Please refer to the photo on page 117 for proof of its comedic value. You say *turkey wattle*, I say *catastrophic neck wound*. I'm telling you, if you think I'm dark and weird and awesome, you should meet my kid!

No matter the exercise, be it physical or mental, your child deserves a bit of supplementary entertainment. And so do you! At the end of the day, when your kid is in her post-gymnastics stupor, drowsy from too many somersaults, begging for her Winnie the Pooh pajamas, and passing out on the couch by 6:00 p.m., you'll be thankful. And that's putting it mildly.

Now go mix yourself a cocktail and watch *The Walking Dead* while you can! What the heck are you waiting for?

You may have to entertain invisible friends.

Before you start wondering if your kid has a disorder, keep in mind imaginary friends are very common. In fact, according to a quote I read from an interview with psychologist Rob Pennington, "Up to 65 percent of children develop an imaginary friend between the ages of 3 and 5." The article continues, "Most children outgrow imaginary friends by the time they go to kindergarten, but about one-third keep them close through age 7."[5]

Those statistics don't surprise me in the least. My brother, Peter, had a whole menagerie of friends when he was a toddler. He often complained his bedtime cohorts, Bert and Ernie from *Sesame Street*, were responsible for making it rain in his room. This never failed to keep him awake all night, so those yahoos *really* should've quit messing with the weather. Pete also had a steady partner in crime, ominously named *The Pacaroni*. I won't pretend to know what the hell a *Pacaroni* is, but I do know he was a rascally chap who got my

---

5 Kim Kyle Morgan, "Imaginary Friends Can Benefit a Child's Brain," *Houston Chronicle*, February 20, 2013, accessed August 1, 2016, http://www.chron.com/news/health/article/Imaginary-friends-can-benefit-a-child-s-brain-4293660.php.

brother into trouble. And since Pete was *by far* the least mischievous child in my family, I'm willing to stick with blaming every mess on that good-for-nothing hooligan. If nothing else, I'm sure Pete appreciates it.

Once, when Gray was nearly four, she got mad at me because I wouldn't allow her imaginary friend to have a brownie before supper.

"But she promises to eat *all* of her dinner!" my daughter whined as her eyes remained single-mindedly fixed on the brownie platter. "It's just one little brownie," she added. A thin trickle of saliva betrayed her by dribbling down her chin.

Honestly? I'd have given her imaginary friend the dang brownie square. Why not? But the trouble with imaginary friends is they share with their not-so-imaginary friends. And while imaginary friends can *totally* handle having sugar before dinner, I know someone else in my house who definitely can't.

I suppose I can't completely count myself out of the imaginary friend equation. When I was two, I had a dream in which my guardian angel made a cameo appearance to inform me my name was supposed to be "Jenna," rather than my given name of "Jennifer." She told me it was her name as well, that I wasn't meant to be called Jennifer, and it was up to me to fix the mistake. Call it what you want—be it divine intervention, an overactive imagination, or the first signs of my lunacy—but I trusted my guardian angel wholeheartedly. The next day I told my parents I would no longer be answering to any name but Jenna. I legally changed it when I turned twelve. Which, by the way, was a decade after my parents gave up on the idea I might ever change it back to Jennifer, whether they liked it or not. I'm nothing if not stubborn.

According to the article I mentioned earlier, "Research shows that children with imaginary friends tend to have above-average vocabulary skills, sharpened cognitive skills, oodles of creativity and

buckets of empathy."[6] Sounds good to me! I'll take whatever validation I can get.

But back to you.

Your kid has imaginary friends? I say invite them over for milk
and cookies. Welcome them in with a handshake and an invisible guest
room. In my house, imaginary friends have an open-door policy. You
know, as long as they don't start levitating the furniture or coaching
my daughters to do disturbing things. Which brings up another point
worth mentioning . . .

Do yourself a favor, and don't confuse the situation by Inter-
net-surfing the subject of "imaginary friends." You're likely to
stumble across some rather twisted explanations for your kid's invisible buddy, which might lead to you hiding in the closet until
someone arrives to shuttle you off in that fashionable ensemble more
commonly referred to as a straitjacket. On the other hand, if your
kid starts methodically collecting the household scissors and chant-
ing *Redrum*, run.

Run and don't look back.

Play that spunky music.

Some kids find their creativity and self-expression in the flow
of melody and lyrics, and I'm all for encouraging that. Who doesn't
love being jolted awake by impromptu song-and-dance routines at
the butt crack of dawn? My own life has been a Broadway musical
just waiting to happen, so it comes as no surprise that my girls are as
drawn to expressing themselves through music as I am.

Maya Angelou has been quoted as saying, "A bird doesn't sing
because it has an answer; it sings because it has a song." This isn't
the case with kids. They don't always sing to present an issue of

---

6 Kim Kyle Morgan, "Imaginary Friends Can Benefit a Child's Brain," *Houston
Chronicle*, February 20, 2013, accessed August 1, 2016, http://www.chron.com/
news/health/article/Imaginary-Friends-Can-Benefit-a-child-s-brain-4293660.php.

substance or express their emotional state. Kids sing because it's fun to rhyme random words like *boob* and *lube*. (Even though they can't possibly understand how creepy those words sound coming out of their mouths.) They sing because they want to explore matching melodies with words like *poop* and *herbivore* or invent three full verses and a chorus about the torture of lima beans. They sing because they want to find a creative way to get back at you for giving them a time-out for that temper tantrum they threw in the middle of Easter dinner. They sing to incorporate lewd lyrics they can't otherwise get away with saying aloud, incorrectly assuming you'll let them off the hook because they're more entertaining than being on laughing gas. Sometimes they sing just to hear themselves make copious amounts of noise.

Make no mistake, your toddler will be sure to perform his dirty little ditty in front of the masses, and it will go on longer than a Jerry Lewis telethon. Kids are charitable like that. If you're extra lucky, it'll be in the waiting room at his pediatrician's office when it's packed. Expect the other waiting parents to smirk and talk about you behind your back, but don't worry—they aren't making fun of you. They're silently thanking God it's happening to *you* today instead of them.

Pro Creation

Despite my playful complaints about the woes of a toddler's imagination and creativity, there are plenty of positive reasons to embrace it too. Here are a few for argument's sake . . . and so you know you aren't in for a future of full-time anarchy.

You don't have to think outside the box.

Boxes are the holy grail of playtime, because kids know how to expertly look past cardboard to the world that lies beyond. While we see the well-worn carton that carried ten pounds of flash-frozen fish sticks and spontaneously purchased kitchenware home from Costco (hello, you foxy Vitamix blender!), our kids see race cars, tropical rainforest canopies, and African safaris. The sky is the limit. How helpful is *that*? It's pretty fantastic when a journey to the center of the earth can take place inside what I generally prefer to think of as *recycling*. Any time my girls are occupied for a few hours by nothing more than a crate and a crayon is fine by me!

One of the coolest things about kids is their unbridled curiosity with banal items we usually take for granted. You name it, they love it! I've seen pots and pans turn into a full orchestra and drink coasters become slices of pizza. There's an exciting adventure in every water bottle, whisk, and straw basket you own. And you know what that means for you? Fun can be found *all around you*. Which means cheap, readily available entertainment in the comfort of your own home. Long live crap camouflaged as craft!

You get to bring your inner child out of hiding.

Who doesn't love to tap into their four-year-old self from time to time? After all, taking a vacation to the land of make-believe can release stress for you too. Sometimes living vicariously through our children's fantasies is just what the doctor ordered.

Somehow I think I never left that special land of make-believe entirely behind me, and I adore traveling back there with Gray and Marlowe. I fondly recall the detective agency my siblings and I built in the closet under the stairs of our childhood home. Some of my favorite memories stem from the afternoons we spent printing fliers and satisfying our mystery-seeking souls. One neighbor even hired us to decode which bird was "stealing" the birdseed from his porch feeder. Two hours later, we were supremely satisfied with our first-rate investigative efforts, and our piggy banks were twenty-five cents richer. Who says a linen closet needs to hold only board games and spare vacuum parts? Sometimes the best thing it holds is an unlimited supply of imagination . . . for your little one *and* you!

It's an excuse to spend more time together.

Let's face it: the best part of getting in on the imagination action with your kids is getting to spend quality time with them. In our house, books are the greatest source of inspiration. My husband, Brad, often schedules Saturday library dates with our girls. They come home with armfuls of reading material they can't wait to flip open, despite the fact that alphabet letters still look like hieroglyphics through their eyes. Books are creativity crack. With *significantly* better health benefits, of course!

When I was a little girl, books took me to faraway places of adventure and intrigue; they offered me an escape through words. Which, I suppose, I can credit for my current career as author. Encouraging your child's mind to dissolve into dreamland on a daily basis can instill a minor fascination that turns into a lifelong passion.

Case in point, Gray is convinced she'll be pursuing a "career" as a princess when she gets older, thanks to the abundance of fairy tale stories we own. Note to self: start working on the dowry for her and Prince George.

Time flies when you're inspired.

This is one of the most bittersweet facets of parenting. It's hard to watch time hurtle past like an asteroid, taking your child's infancy along with it. Then again, it's great when time flies during that nine-hour car ride to Grandma's house so you don't spend the entire trip clawing at the sunroof and dreaming of scenes from *Throw Momma from the Train.* I wonder if the term *claustrophobia* was fabricated by some poor, frazzled, exhausted mommy who endeavored to take a road trip with her five kids. Ah, the joys of traveling with children.

When it comes down to it, your kids will grow up faster than you want them to. But it leads to some pretty cool milestones! Before you know it, you'll be graduating from watching your child *lick* the box of crayons to watching her break that box open and draw something you can hang on the refrigerator. Who cares if it looks like a phallic hot air balloon? Next stop: crudely constructed bow tie pasta frames and kiln-fired ceramic ashtrays. Even if no one smokes in your house but burnt breakfast toast.

Nurturing creativity means you're fostering dreams.

The energy and time it takes to support your toddler's creativity will come back to you tenfold. Someday your baby will go to college all the way across the country and come home only for holiday weekends so you can do her laundry. Then you'll finally have some peace and quiet. Just kidding.

Someday the imagination you've encouraged will lead your dreamer out of the town he was raised in to explore that big, beautiful world out there. He might pursue a passion for archaeology or a career in the culinary arts. Or maybe the voyage itself will be the ambition! Perhaps your daughter will send postcards from every piazza she paints in Italy, join a nonprofit to save the tigers in Tibet, or traverse the Great Wall of China in suction cup shoes à la Spider-Man. That's when you'll realize all the ingenuity and artistry you fostered contribute to the larger picture.

So make another pot of coffee (or five) and keep on trucking!

THE MORAL OF MY STORY

Nurturing my girls' imagination and creativity is a crazy, wonderful, exhausting, constant endeavor. Just when I think I'm done building Lego skyscrapers, decorating my husband's desk in fire hydrant stickers, constructing a Mr. T mosaic out of Post-it notes, and designing wedding dresses made entirely of toilet paper, they beg me to finger paint zebra stripes on the dogs or make a papier-mâché mask of my mother-in-law. But I love every minute of our artistic adventures! Even when they keep me from returning work e-mails, getting an extra hour of sleep, or cleaning the house. Especially cleaning the house.

Now, go put on that unicorn costume your kid just handed you and repeat your new mantra: *I'm a creativity gladiator!*

Potty training has to start somewhere . . . The mind-blowing intrigue of
toilet paper captures Marlowe's attention first.
Photo courtesy of Jenna von Oy.

CHAPTER 7

Potty Training . . . It's a Crap Shoot

A SCENIC VIEW OF MY PAST

Years ago, I took a trip to Napa Valley with one of my dearest long-time friends, JD. I'd been mulling over the idea of driving up North by myself on a weeklong "soul vacation" (to nurture the bruised ego left behind from a breakup I should've been celebrating instead of mourning), so when I received an invitation to the Harvest Celebration at a froufrou, über-elite Napa Winery— let's just say the name rhymes with Opus One—I thought, *Postbreakup merrymaking and free booze? How could I go wrong?*

Actually, that's not the whole story. I fancy myself a mildly knowledgeable wine connoisseur, so I geeked out over the opportunity to taste vintages that were older (and had likely aged better) than me. And boy, did I ever taste them! But I'm getting way ahead of myself.

First, I should explain how JD entered the picture. JD—who's *far* funnier and cleverer than I'll ever be—and I go back to a time when I hosted a humble Nashville-meets-flashy-Hollywood guitar party, at my old house in the hills of Encino, California. Essentially, a bunch of Nashville singer-songwriters congregated in my living room and used their talent to knock the damn socks off some Los Angeles industry folks. It was an awesome display. Those agent/actor types might've been expecting a posse of backwoods Tennessee rednecks with banjos and giant belt buckles, but they changed their tune rather quickly. Pun very much intended.

Let's get back to how JD and I became such close friends. This might sound strange, but JD and I bonded the morning after my country music house party over our discovery of one of my guests skinny-dipping in my pool. For the record, you ain't seen nothin' until you've woken up (bleary-eyed and hungover) to a naked Nash-villian worshipping the California sun whilst doing poolside yoga. Stumbling upon a virtual stranger in his birthday suit before you've even downed your first cup of coffee is a more festive awakening than anyone really needs on any given morning. Or wants. (Or deserves, depending on his physique.) As an aside, in case you're contemplating trying this at home, a bare ass doesn't gracefully lend itself to most yoga poses. I'm with JD, who quipped, "If he does downward dog, I'm outta here."

And that's the remark that officially solidified our friendship. Yep, we owe our companionship to a set of clothing-deficient, med-itation-happy, Nashville-based buns.

Back to the Napa winery story. When the invitation arrived kindly requesting my presence at an exclusive shindig honoring high-end winemakers offering a smorgasbord of free food and alcohol, I RSVPed faster than Martha Stewart's personal etiquette guru. I may also have jumped up and down, squealed like a Maroon 5 fangirl, and run around in circles like a puppy chasing its tail. Who knows? It was a long time ago. What I *do* know is when JD called and joked about joining me on Operation Inebriation, I thought, *Why wouldn't I bring along a travel buddy and booze-guzzling ally?*

The next thing I knew, we were vineyard bound.

In advance of our journey to Wino's Wonderland . . . I mean, Napa Valley . . . I went online to secure a place to stay. Napa is quaint, so the idea of a bed and breakfast was appealing. As luck would have it, I found a perfect garden-view getaway that still had rooms available. It was well over three hundred dollars a night, but I told my wallet to quit complaining, and I jumped on it.

After a nine-hour drive from Los Angeles, which included mind-numbing rush-hour traffic through San Francisco, we were relieved to reach our destination.

Relieved, that is, until we actually saw the place.

Pulling into the driveway of the B&B, we bucked and bounced over gravel studded with deep potholes. Where was our elegant sign? Where was the impeccably mowed lawn and manicured hedges? More importantly, where was the charming cottage with the inviting entryway? There wasn't even a mailbox. And a lovely, lush garden view? Only if parking lots count. The yard was sparsely decorated in crabgrass, with an exquisite smattering of dandelions. On the other hand, if we were in need of car parts, we'd hit the jackpot; it was a mechanic's mecca up in that joint. Well, if any of those hunks of junk were destined to come off their cinder blocks. Which I sincerely doubted.

JD and I eyed each other with skepticism bordering on fear.

"Thank God *you're* the one who found this place," he murmured, "or I'd never hear the end of it."

I was too speechless to argue. Plus, he was correct. He'd seriously lucked out by letting me micromanage our trip details. After all, we had to drive *back* to Los Angeles at some point, and nine hours is an awfully long time for a man to be nagged about a supposedly swanky B&B that looks more like the Bates Motel.

"Maybe the inside is beautiful," JD said in a tone that said exactly the opposite.

Heading in, we slipped into our best positive attitudes but brought our sarcasm along just in case.

No one was around. Let me rephrase that: No one of legal age to check us in was around. Instead, a little girl greeted us like she ran the place. I briefly wondered if social services knew there was a five-year-old concierge handing out room keys at a so-called bed and breakfast in Northern Cali.

My imagination began scampering off to preposterous, faraway places. I pondered whether our new friend was really a seventy-year-old, chain-smoking receptionist cleverly disguised as an innocent, pigtailed ruffian. Or maybe she'd accidentally stumbled upon the fountain of youth in her weed-infested backyard, and she'd done too much splashing around in the water. Who knows?

Behind our new little friend, massive stacks of newspapers decorated the dining room. Apparently the *breakfast* portion of our *bed and breakfast* was brought to us by back issues of the San Francisco Chronicle.

That's when we spotted the resident "adult." He was curled up on the tattered couch, spooning a giant mastiff and taking a midday nap. They were snoring in tandem.

JD and I exchanged looks that silently screamed, *What the heck have we gotten ourselves into?* but with HBO language.

Against our better judgment, we asked the youngster where we might find our room. I'd already paid the deposit, so . . . couldn't we drink enough to successfully forget how heinous our accommodations were?

The answer to that question is *No. No, we couldn't.* Any hope we had evaporated once we got to our room and saw the creepy-ass porcelain Mardi Gras dolls reclining on the bed. Oh yeah, and the bathroom door that wouldn't shut enough for us to urinate in private, which is a serious problem when you're traveling with a friend *without* benefits.

As it happens, there wasn't enough wine on the West Coast to overcome the fact that Li'l Miss Five-Year-Old clung to me like a

Bounce fabric softener sheet for the next hour (nobody came looking for her), or that the plush beds we were expecting felt more like Astroturf from a minigolf fairway. Don't get me wrong, that isn't to say we didn't give the whole concept of *drinking ourselves into a state of fathomless oblivion* the old college try. We made sure our new friend was in the custody of her guardian, escaped to that winery quicker than you can say, "Pinot noir," drank until we'd reached the pinnacle of our wine-consumption capabilities, then cabbed it back to our scary digs for what we knew would be the *only* night we attempted to stay there. Provided, of course, those Mardi Gras dolls didn't come to life in the wee hours and stab us in our sleep like Chuckie.

In the morning, I awoke to the absence of JD. I figured my friend couldn't have gone very far, because I had the car keys. But what could he possibly be doing? Picking dandelions? Alphabetizing newspaper stacks? Sewing homemade voodoo dolls to add to the collection?

I found him by the pool in a rickety plastic chair, working on the novel he was writing. He looked up at me with an expression I translated to, *Save me.*

"This is Brutus," he informed me, motioning to the gargantuan mastiff sawing logs nearby. "I came out here to enjoy the peaceful morning, and Brutus promptly joined me. Even better, he introduced himself by dropping a giant, steamy poop on my shoe."

That was the last straw. We booked it out of there and let them keep our deposit money. They clearly needed it more than we did.

CUT TO . . .

You can drink away a solitary night of Mardi Gras dolls, newspaper hoarding, defecating mastiffs, and eternally open bathroom doors; that's child's play. You know what you *can't* drink away? Potty training your kid. Welcome to purgatory.

MY CRADLE CHRONICLES

I once received a Twitter message from a fan that read, "Potty training should include a care package with gloves, bleach, multiple bottles of wine, and an emergency Xanax scrip." She left out a few crucial items, but Twitter only allows for a measly 150 characters. I'd add a couple of essentials, namely a hazmat suit, a lifetime supply of air freshener, and waterproof pads for every piece of furniture you own. This includes, but isn't limited to, your bed, couch, dining room chairs, and any rug you can't force-feed to your washing machine.

It's also helpful to have a trove of bribe-related goodies on hand, whether you poo-poo the idea of bribing or not. As I've mentioned, I normally try to avoid bribing, but for the love of God, a woman needs a backup plan! If you're feeling exceptionally enterprising, you may also wish to soundproof your bathroom. You know, so none of your neighbors call the cops when it sounds like you're inflicting some unimaginable horror on your child, even though you've merely suggested he sit on the toilet instead of squatting behind the sofa to take a crap in his brand-new Batman undies.

Despite your comprehensive cache of antimess, antistench, and antilunacy remedies, you may find you aren't prepared for the tumultuous nature of getting your child beyond the diaper-wearing phase. Dare I say, *Shit happens?*

Let's get this potty started.

I'll begin with a potty-related story of my own. When I was about six years old, I did a commercial for Northern Bathroom Tissue. In it, I was riding my bike on a treacherously bumpy sidewalk, wincing in pain, and rubbing my poor, bruised bottom in misery. My character rode all the way to the local market, where she purchased a giant roll of toilet tissue and proceeded to shove it down her pants as a bicycle seat buffer. She then rode home in all her comfortable, paper-padded (and, oh, so fat-bottomed) splendor.

That ad campaign was a very memorable introduction to the bizarre notoriety my booty has acquired over the years, but at least I got paid for it! Thanks to Northern Bathroom Tissue, my big ass was famous early on. People used to stop me on the street and inquire if I was "the girl from that commercial who stuffed toilet paper down her pants." Which thrilled me ever so much since, as one can imagine, that's something every kid wants to be known for.

I hope, for your sake, your child doesn't incite such public discussions about his bathroom business. In a sense, that begins with you.

Don't worry, pee happy.

The start of your adventures in toileting can be slow going. Don't expect overnight success! As with crawling, walking, talking, and every other significant milestone we parents await with bated breath, potty training will happen in due time. But first, there's a lot of sweating, crying, hair pulling, uncontrollable twitching, and occasional foaming at the mouth. And that's just on your end! My advice? Try not to press the issue. If your infant or toddler is showing interest in testing the waters, go for it. Set him up on the chair and see what happens. But I encourage you to tread lightly. In my experience, when potty training feels like an obligation, kids respond less enthusiastically. In fact, it can make a toddler who's curious about training suddenly decide he's scared of it.

I know you may have a deadline rattling around in your brain—most of us do. You may even have a day care deadline that dictates your child can't graduate to the next classroom if she's not potty trained. Regardless, I still stand by the *don't push* approach. It'll be worth the wait when the transition isn't rockier than Mt. Rushmore.

It's important not to base your child's potty-training timeline on "standards" offered by family, friends, or the Internet. It can be a lengthy, discouraging process if your child isn't physically and emotionally ready for it.

As parents, some of our motivation to start potty training comes from a selfish place. We might want to get rid of the dirty diaper pails, ill-timed blowouts, and inadvertent trail of stench through every aisle of Whole Foods. I've been there. It's a bit of a bummer when your fellow grocery store patrons can't decide if that rotten, gamy smell is your baby or the expired Gorgonzola.

We want to encourage our kids to grow, and potty training is one of those big steps toward independence and maturity. But I hope you'll heed my warning if you're met with resistance. Some kids need a little extra time before they're ready to handle the act of expelling bodily fluids into a catch basin. Not to mention, it's followed by the push of a button that noisily and abruptly vacuums everything into the earth. When you think of it that way, it's not hard to imagine why that might seem a wee bit scary to a tiny human!

Minor confusion ensues as Gray tries on her princess undies for the first time.
Photo courtesy of Jenna von Oy.

The princess and the pee.

If it helps, I'll tell you a bit about how we potty trained our first daughter, Gray. I realize your experience will differ from mine, but sometimes it's nice to hear an example or two. You never know what you can glean from someone else's trial and error!

We bought Gray a mini potty chair when she was just over a year old. It was just her size, which allowed her to climb on without help. We set it in the bathroom alongside our bigger commode, explained its purpose, and put a few *Everyone Poops*–type books next to it for added entertainment value. Doesn't everyone enjoy a little bathroom reading? After that, we completely ignored the whole shebang until Gray expressed interest. Essentially, we introduced the concept without forcing her to take part in it.

As I suspected, curiosity got the better of her. I soon found her sitting on it—fully clothed and flipping through *Elmo's Potty Time*. I asked if she wanted to try going to the bathroom on the "big-girl chair," and she nodded. I don't think she fully grasped the idea at that point, but it was a good first step! I removed her diaper and set her back down.

Now, I know you think this is heading somewhere exciting, so let me burst that bubble . . . Nothing happened.

When she started to climb off the chair, I put her diaper back on. She defiled said diaper not ten seconds later, and I changed it. End of mind-blowing story.

But you know what? Sometimes *not* peeing in the toilet teaches just as much of a lesson as peeing in it. They have to start somewhere! That day, my daughter began learning what the potty chair was for, even if there weren't immediate results.

It took a while before Gray really understood the point of the potty or wanted to sit on it for reasons other than its novelty, but eventually we recognized clear signs she was ready for the next step.

That's when the true training process really began. That Christmas, Santa gifted her with princess panties. You're probably thinking, *What two-year-old gives a crumb about unwrapping underwear?* But you'd be surprised at how persuasive those Disney princesses can be. Who knew they would wind up being my daughter's most influential diaper-ditching allies? As soon as Gray pulled on a pair of those undies, it was *Good-bye, diapers; hello, wads of toilet tissue shoved carelessly into the toilet bowl.*

Ultimately, I look back on our training endeavors as being relatively quick and easy. We came, we saw, we potty trained.

I almost feel bad for admitting it was such a breeze. *Almost.* After the countless horror stories I'd heard, I'd anticipated jumping through more hoops than a poodle at the Westminster dog show. I thought I'd be praying for spiked eggnog by the time it was all said and done. But lo and behold, there's no accounting for the fierce determination of a little girl who wants to wear her new Cinderella bloomers.

To recap, I clearly wasn't the mastermind behind some brilliant training tactic that tricked my toddler into thinking the bathroom was a magical emporium of wonder and excitement. I give all the credit to Gray, who made up her mind and never looked back. I simply played my part as purveyor of princess panties, postpotty hand-washing helper, cheer squad, and proud mommy. For the most part, that's the best any of us can do.

It's my potty and I'll cry if I want to.

Let's jump back into the potty-training trenches for a minute. At some irksome and logic-violating juncture, you may find the training progress hits a wall . . . A giant, impenetrable, tear-stained, brick wall. In other words, sometimes your child takes a few steps back. *Way* back. As in, she's crying and screaming in the corner, pointing at the toilet like it's about to jump up and bite her cherubic little bum. That isn't out of the ordinary, and I once again go back to—it's best not to force anything. Your kid won't head to high school in Pampers, I promise! It's perfectly okay to feel a bit disgruntled by the slow pace, and you probably will at some point. I had my moments too. But I urge you to give your child space to return to the training on his time, rather than yours. Kids tend to better absorb ideas when they're under the impression they've come up with them on their own! (P.S. Sometimes that works on husbands too.)

The truth is, sometimes kids lose interest or rebel a little; sometimes the idea of sitting on the potty chair loses its novelty or "fun" factor. When I was just shy of two, I was fully toilet trained. Not too long after, I found out my best friend was still in diapers. I informed my mom that I, too, was going back to wearing diapers until John was out of them. Fortunately, my mom was smart and patient enough to know it was just a passing phase. It lasted for a short time, and then I returned to my big-girl underpants without a second thought.

I briefly experienced a similar lapse in progress with Gray. Even after she'd had a few "Hallelujah, can I get a witness?" training moments, she went through a stage during which she wanted nothing to do with it. And by that I mean she wouldn't step foot in the bathroom and took off running as soon as her diaper was removed. This led me to a few hot dates with Mr. Clean, mopping up piddle puddles together. Which brings up another important point . . .

The accidental toiletist.

It's critical to make sure your child doesn't feel ashamed by accidents. We all make mistakes while learning something new! I'm not suggesting you'd punish your kid for soiling his diaper, but sometimes we instinctively jump to our *Oh, crap, what have you done?* face. It's not always easy to catch oneself midreaction and transition to a positive reinforcement such as, "Accidents happen. Let's try sitting on the potty now, in case you aren't done yet." and/or "Don't forget to tell me when you have to go potty so I can help you get there in time."

When Gray had accidents, I discovered they bothered her far more than they bothered me. Truth be told, they totally freaked her out; she's kind of a perfectionist that way. During those moments, my most important mommy job became helping her let herself off the hook. Thankfully, she quickly learned to shake it off and say, "Mommy, I had a little accident, but that's okay because you can clean it up." And I always did—along with that special bald buddy we were talking about earlier, of course. He's one hell of a housekeeper! I'm telling you, if Mr. Clean could also babysit, he'd be the world's perfect guy.

Gray had only a handful of accidents at the very beginning of her toilet training, but who knows if Marlowe will follow suit? A friend recently told me her kids have had accidents for years, especially overnight. Your child may also go without an accident for a bit and then suddenly have several in a row. This is especially common when there are changes in the normal routine you've set. I know someone whose son had gone over a year with no accident of any kind, then randomly defecated in the middle of his grandparents' living room not five minutes after they'd arrived for a weekend visit.

When there are schedule changes, periods of major transition, or your child is overstimulated, it's not difficult to see how he might ignore his body's need for a bathroom. Hell, when I'm busy, even I tend to hold it until I'm doing an interpretive dance. (Yes, I realize how bad that is for my body. I'll work on it. At least I don't get as far as losing my bowels and messing up my *Dora the Explorer* undies! Not that I own any. That would be a little freaky.)

Teach your child to be up front about his bathroom needs, but don't be surprised when he isn't. And invest in a wet-vac.

Take pee-cautionary measures.

As I mentioned earlier, potty training takes some getting used to. Your son might be watching Saturday morning cartoons and decide he doesn't feel like waiting until the commercial break to hit up the bathroom, so he pees all over himself and the sofa while laughing at the anvil that just pummeled Road Runner's head. Or your daughter might forget she hasn't worn diapers for the last three weeks and suddenly yell, "Mommy, I think I peed on the floor." She *thinks*. You know, because that pond she's currently wading in wasn't enough of a sign. And if you have boys? They notoriously hold their urine for too long. I was at a friend's house when I overheard her say to her son, "Get in that bathroom right now. You're going to lose your schmeckel if you keep holding that much urine in it!" I laughed until I almost peed myself.

You obviously can't protect every item you own from errant tinkle streams, unless you cover everything in tacky plastic slipcovers like your Great-Aunt Bea. In the name of style and class, I don't recommend going that route. There are, however, a few things you can buy to make your life easier and less urine-soaked. Your furniture will appreciate the backup plan.

1. Get a waterproof mattress cover—for your child's bed and for yours.
Picture this: It's the middle of the night and you're sleeping peacefully. In fact, you're experiencing a beautiful dream in which you're enjoying a little hot tub hanky-panky with Channing Tatum. The dream begins to dissipate as you're aroused from slumber (in more ways than one). Suddenly, you realize you're actually wet. What the hell? It takes a moment to figure out your child has migrated from her bed to yours, and that steamy hot tub water is actually pee.

The carbon monoxide alarm would be a less jarring wake-up call.

If you have a waterproof mattress cover, you can throw your sheets and the cover in the hamper, put fresh linens on the bed, move your kid back to her own room, and go back to sleep in under ten minutes. The only thing that cover can't do is help you get Channing back. You're on your own with that one.

2. A wee pad for your couch—or wherever else it's needed . . . Like everywhere.

Even though Gray didn't have accidents often, we kept a waterproof pad (I'm particularly fond of the Conni Kids wee pad) on our couch for the first month or two after she'd been trained. Why tempt fate? Couch cushions aren't always easy to clean, and they see enough crayon drawings, melted chocolate stains, saliva-laden Cheerio mush, and dog hair as it is. Why not spare them the additional drama?

3. Pull-ups.

I'll start by saying these never worked for us. For many kids, they bridge the gap between diaper and underwear, convincing children to pay closer attention to their urges.

In my older daughter's case, pull-ups still felt too much like a diaper, so she didn't bother making bathroom trips at all while wearing them. And since they aren't meant to retain the same level of moisture as a diaper, they weren't terribly effective. Still, I believe they have a place in the training process for some kids. Since I currently have a closet shelf full of the pull-ups Gray never touched, I'll let you know how it goes with Marlowe.

Dream a little dream of pee.

Whether you want to or not, you'll wind up doing a few less-than-refined things you've never dreamed of (and never wanted to) while potty training your child, and you'll think nothing of it. In other words, things that seemed gross in your single-girl days will suddenly seem as uneventful as a Barry Manilow concert. For example, you might hear the phrase "Mom, my bottom hurts; can you pick my underwear out?" at which point you'll absentmindedly head over to extricate said wedgie while simultaneously deliberating the merits of buying organic lettuce.

In honor of this concept, I'd like to butcher a beautiful poem by Emma Lazarus. "Give me your turd, your poo; your huddled masses yearning to be free; the wretched refuse . . ." Okay, okay, I'll stop there. I know—you'll never think of the Statue of Liberty in quite the same way, right? Sorry about that. Sort of. I simply couldn't resist taking a little "poo-etic" license. I swear I'm done now. The fact is, once you've been peed on, pooped on (you can go ahead and preemptively cross *that* off your bucket list), belched on, and farted on by your potty-training toddler, nothing will faze you anymore.

For all the board game lovers out there, you can also play a pretty mean game of bathroom bingo with all the events I just mentioned.

The life of the potty.

Toddlers tend to develop interesting and unexpected evacuation habits as they perfect their potty proficiency. For example, I have a friend who caught her son pissing in Cheerios so he could practice his aim. How industrious!

He's not alone. Gray once told me, "My hair's getting so long, pretty soon it'll fall into the toilet and I'll have to pee in the sink instead." Clever rationale there, kid.

Here's a rundown of some of the unique potty-training quirks you might have to look forward to . . .

1. *Toddlers never remember to flush the toilet.* I'm serious. Never.

People are struck by lightning more often than your kid will flush. Consequently, your bathroom may end up smelling like hamster vomit with a side of blue cheese. Make sure you give all bathrooms a once-over before your boss comes over for dinner. It's also a good idea to double-check the toilet bowl before you let your nosy dog have free rein of the house. Ew.

2. *Toddlers get obsessed with shoving mass quantities of paper down the toilet vortex.* For some unknown reason, children are fascinated by the idea of stuffing the toilet like it's a Thanksgiving turkey. Ah, the mystery and intrigue of tissue dissolving in urine. It's packed with more action than the last few Nic Cage films. Actually, that's less of a joke than it should be. Anyway, be wary of long stretches of silence while your kid is behind closed lavatory doors. It likely means you're losing your Cottonelle rolls to the soggy abyss. My daughter has constructed many a papier-mâché pyramid in our commode. And since mounds of wet tissue in a toilet tend to cause an environmental disaster reminiscent of the Exxon Valdez spill, you might want to nip that in the bud. Or butt, as the case may be.

3. *Kids feel the need for treats when they successfully poop in the potty.* Some moments are teachable moments, some are bribing moments, and some are both. For argument's sake, we'll take the "evil" out of bribing by referring to it as *rewarding* in this instance, but you and I know the truth. This ain't our first rodeo.

When dealing with brib—sorry, *rewarding,* it's important to know kids aren't generally satisfied with a gold star or sticker handout for a successful trip to the powder room. I even have a girlfriend who kept a shoe box of dollar store toys on a shelf in the linen closet. In my house, toys were less effective. For reasons far beyond my comprehension (and I'd like to keep it that way), my children appear to associate pooping with getting chocolate. My daughters are more motivated by a single M&M than by any other celebratory offering. I prefer confetti and a bottle of champagne myself, but . . .

Potty-training rewards have always been my exception to the rule on bribing. I respect if they aren't yours, but I sort of delighted in doling out special treats in honor of my new career as baby bottom wiper. Of course, when my kid started bargaining for extra candy if she went "above and beyond" by washing her hands too, I had to rethink my methods. Yeesh. You give kids an inch, they'll take your yardstick and run around the house chasing dogs with it.

4. Bed-wetting isn't uncommon. I don't know that this necessarily qualifies as a "quirk," but it's still worth mentioning. Bed-wetting isn't something we've dealt with in our house, so I can't speak to it with any firsthand knowledge. I do, however, have several friends who've had to work through this issue with one child or more, and here's one key factor I gleaned—nighttime accidents happen way more often when kids drink water or milk before bed. Granted, that's not the only cause for bed-wetting, but it's worth noting.

Bed-wetting can be a serious source of frustration because it can occur even after a child is fully toilet trained. According to the Mayo Clinic, "Most kids are fully toilet trained by age 5, but there's really no target date for developing complete bladder control. Between the ages of 5 and 7, bed-wetting remains a problem for some children. After 7 years of age, a small number of children still wet the bed."[7] I realize this may mean the light is at the end of a very long tunnel, involving endless laundry and oodles of cleaning supplies, but at least you know your kid is normal! There's nothing for you *or* your little one to feel ashamed about if bed-wetting is an issue.

---

7 "Bed-wetting symptoms," Mayo Clinic, accessed August 1, 2016, http://www.mayoclinic.org/diseases-conditions/bed-wetting/basics/symptoms/con-20015089.

5. *To a child, poop doubles as paint.* If this is news to you, and especially if you have a boy, be prepared for a few masterful mosaics of manure.

One night my good friend discovered her son had finger painted his bedroom walls. "When I left him, he was lying down quietly," she told me. "When I returned, he'd actually pulled off his own diaper, taken out the poo, and gone to town all over the fool place. That's when we got serious about potty training."

Kids are stealthy. In a spur-of-the-moment demonstration of boredom-initiated bathroom graffiti, motivated by the psychic guidance of Basquiat, you might return to find your formerly pristine tiles coated in a thick layer of turd. Your jaw will hit the ground with the impact of a meteor, the abominable stench will assault your nose, and you'll struggle to form words that don't land squarely in the cussing category. I'd tell you to start by taking a deep breath to steady yourself, but . . . taking any sort of breath at all isn't advisable in that scenario.

Eat, drink, and pee merry. But make sure those three activities take place before *a car ride.*

My final point, before abandoning this crude subject altogether, is probably the most important one: Always make sure your kid goes to the bathroom before getting in the car. Even if he complains he doesn't have to go, and even if he throws a fit loud enough to be heard in Botswana.

Kids have bladders the size of a gumdrop, so it's not always easy for them to "hold it" for any length of time. By the time your son informs you of his need for a restroom, it's already an urgent matter. Take my word on that. You can try distracting him with games like I Spy or Car Bingo, but you're on borrowed time. Postponing a bathroom run is like convincing yourself you can dismantle a bomb before it detonates. You'll spend the next seven minutes uneasily glancing at your child in the rearview mirror while desperately hoping a McDonald's will jump out at you and scream, "I have an empty and (relatively) clean bathroom!"

With boys, it's significantly easier to pull over on exit eleven for a discreet spot to water a patch of grass. Little girls tend to be more particular about their surroundings and the presence of toilet paper. Can you blame them? Here are a few suggestions to help you avoid the stress of potential vehicular urinicide.

1. It seems obvious, but get in the habit of always *making your kid potty before leaving the house.* It doesn't matter if it's a two-hour excursion to the beach or a two-minute trip to the bank.

You're the only person who's going to enforce the Don't Wait to Urinate rule, so any and all forethought is up to you. Your kid won't think of it until the house is locked up, there's a seat belt pressed against her bladder, and you're just far enough from home she can't make it back before soaking her seat. God help you if you have to get on gravel roads or a street riddled with potholes before a bathroom is in sight, because you can't throw car seats in the washing machine, and you probably didn't pack an extra set of clothing for a jaunt down the street. Which leads me to . . .

2. Keep a travel potty in your car. We have the Kalencom 2-in-1 Potette Plus, which comes complete with liner bags. In a pinch, it can even be lined with plastic grocery bags.

The minipotty has saved us on many occasions when Gray has spontaneously declared, "Mommy, I need to go potty right *now!*" You might ask how I've wound up in this predicament if I successfully practice what I preach by making my kids use the bathroom before leaving the house. The answer is pretty cut-and-dried, though technically there's nothing dry about it. I don't always remember to follow my own advice. Ah, the hypocrisy of it all! And because Murphy is a law-abiding bastard, this always manages to occur three miles from any sort of restroom-bearing establishment I would consider stepping foot in, much less allowing one of my daughters to enter. Instead, the travel potty allows for privacy, the safety of remaining in our car, and immediate relief for my kid. Even if trying to help her get on a toilet in the backseat of my vehicle requires being more limber than anyone should be.

3. Put a waterproof cover on your toddler's car seat. We're not talking about some jumbo contraption that looks like you've outfitted your backseat in a rain slicker; it's just a small, square, absorbent piece that fits right underneath your child's bottom. It's a precautionary piddle pad, and it's a no-brainer—inexpensive, simple to install, and an efficient, easily washable barrier against any blowout shy of Old Faithful!

THE MORAL OF MY STORY

No two children are identical, so no two potty-training paths are the same. The whole endeavor will require the patience of Mother Teresa and all the saints, but one day your kid will be walking around diaperless and fancy-free. But hopefully not pants-free.

Rub-a-dub-dub, Marlowe's sitting in the tub . . . fully clothed.
Photo courtesy of Jenna von Oy.

CHAPTER 8

Surviving the Health Nuts

A SCENIC VIEW OF MY PAST

During my single-girl days, when I was feeling particularly saucy, I would don my spikiest stilettos and join my fabulous friend Justin (who I fondly refer to as Justina) for a fun night out on the town in West Hollywood. By *fun*, I mean debaucherous. There's nothing quite like dancing the night away at a gay club with a guy in diamond-studded fishnets. Especially when said guy walks through the door and men shout his name like he's Adonis while rushing to give him free cocktails, the majority of which *you* wind up drinking. Also noteworthy—I've even been on the receiving end of an ass grab or two, courtesy of simply standing next to him. We'll call that *sexploitation by association*. Needless to say, going out with Justina can be an interesting social experiment.

One evening when we were in our twenties, Justina and I decided to get all gussied up and cause a little ruckus. We cruised to his favorite bar, downed a few cosmopolitans, chatted up some cute boys—who were clearly uninterested in the straight girl who was inadvertently cockblocking—and danced with reckless abandon. Or at the very least, with a sizable buzz.

Things really heated up when the karaoke started. I sang "Like a Virgin," which tends to be a crowd pleaser, but you ain't seen nothin' until you've seen Justina do his cover of Tina Turner's "Proud Mary."

It's a showstopper—an adventurous musical extravaganza of seismic proportions that culminates in a confetti explosion of bar napkins. I've seen Broadway shows less entertaining. In fact, the only things he was missing were pyrotechnics and a national tour. Suffice it to say we painted the town red that night, though with Justina's flare for the dramatic I suspect he would've preferred chartreuse.

We finally made it back to his place in the early morning hours, having managed to procure a pocketful of phone numbers, sore feet, a few miscellaneous bruises from overzealous dancing, a silvery feather boa, and one random sequined sombrero we had no recollection of acquiring. Thank God we weren't doing tequila shooters in Tijuana; God only knows *what* we might've come home with. Knowing us, we would've tried to smuggle a burro back across the border.

The next morning, after two pots of coffee that didn't make a dent in our headaches, we decided to go on a shopping excursion. I don't know if you know this, but nothing cures the woozies quite like buying a new set of dishes you don't need. It's the new hair of the dog, and it's all the rage . . . at least that's what my warped little twentysomething inner voice convinced me of.

We jumped into Justina's Jag (read: slowly and carefully climbed in so as to avoid spontaneous vomiting) and ventured to the Century City mall. I hid behind a baseball cap and oversized Jackie O. sunglasses and fervently prayed the hangover gods would have mercy on my soul. Also, that I wouldn't run into any casting directors or network execs while I was such a lovely, queasy shade of green. Per usual, Justina was dressed to impress in obscenely short shorts and knee-high boots that looked like he'd skinned a Sasquatch. Good thing we weren't attracting attention in our inconspicuous getups.

Stopping at a designer boutique, I eyed a dress that might ease some of my pain. Justina looked at me knowingly, nodded his approval, and we sashayed up to the checkout counter together, merchandise in hand. What we saw there obliterated our delirium in mere seconds: Bending down to retrieve a shopping bag was the most beautiful specimen of a man we'd ever seen . . . complete with Superman tighty-whities clearing the waistband of his jeans. Dumbfounded, Justina opened his mouth to say something.

"Don't," I whispered, cutting him off. "Let's not ruin the moment."

"I wonder if he likes sombreros," Justina whispered back.

What's my point in all of this, you ask? It's that there can be a fine line between agony and nirvana . . . Sometimes all you need to cure your ills is the sight of Superman underwear on a well-defined, masculine bum.

P.S. It might also be worth mentioning that one is better off leaving a dance club with a few more of one's faculties intact and a few less cosmopolitans in one's bloodstream. But never leave behind the sequined sombrero. You never know when it might come in handy.

CUT TO . . .

That line between agony and nirvana gets even finer when you have kids, especially as it pertains to concepts such as personal hygiene. If I thought all-night drunk dancing at a gay club left me physically taxed, it was nothing compared to how weary I feel every time I'm tasked with brushing my daughter's teeth. And don't get me started on bath time! Even a sequined sombrero does me no good on that one. Which is truly a shame.

MY CRADLE CHRONICLES

Personal hygiene can be a tough issue for parents, and I'm using the term *tough* pretty loosely here. Namely, this is because a two-year-old (or three-year-old or four-year-old) doesn't give a flying turd about whether or not she has worse breath than a campground Porta-Potty, hair that suggests she took styling lessons from a cockatoo, or feet that make the inside of her sneakers smell like dried peaches. Toddlers are notorious for forgetting to wash their hands after a trip to the bathroom (where they undoubtedly caressed every inch of the toilet), farting and belching at the most inopportune moments (such as directly in the face of the store owner at one's very first book signing in Los Angeles—thank you, Marlowe!), and wiping a trail of slimy snot on their shirtsleeves.

Toddlers also have a penchant for running toward oncoming traffic as if they've hallucinated a humongous ice cream sundae on the opposite sidewalk, and for chatting it up with every Tom, Dick, and Harriette with whom they cross paths . . . even when that person sends your hackles up faster than an American flag on Memorial Day. (More on that in the next chapter.)

The fact is, children learn to take safety precautions and practice healthful living by following your example, being encouraged to have good sanitation habits, learning their actions have consequences, and developing a routine over time. But before all that happens, they're a grimy, germ-infested, disheveled disaster.

Thank God they're so lovable.

Hygiene High Jinks Ensue

Here are a few topics that might shed some light on what you're in for—aside from an avalanche of dirt and bacteria—while attempting to teach your toddler the basics of personal hygiene.

Beware of uncontrolled substances.

Toddlers have no germ control awareness, and they attract viruses like cockroaches to a seedy Vegas motel. If you have a kid in day care, you can amend that to read: cockroaches at a seedy Vegas motel where someone left behind a doggie bag from the all-you-can-eat grease-palooza down the street. Or worse. For this reason, pretty please don't send your kid to school with a fever. A runny nose you pass off as late-onset teething or seasonal allergies? Sure, I get it—I'm a mom with needs too. How else would you have time to fold the towering mounds of laundry? Or watch this season of *The Blacklist?*

A leaky, snotty nose is par for the course, and schools expect that more than they expect your kid to actually sleep during structured naptime. But seriously—keep your kid home if he has bodily fluids coming out of both ends, a fever, and/or a rash that's prominent enough to keep his classmates busy playing connect-the-dots during recess.

Here are a few suggestions for helping to keep your child (and everyone else in a ten-mile radius) from being a walking, talking phlegm factory.

1. Teach your toddler to cover coughs and sneezes. Kids don't automatically know to cough into their elbow or hand when they're sick, and you'll spend an absurd amount of time keeping after them about it. You'll probably have to repeat yourself a few thousand times before it actually resonates, provided it ever does. In fact, at some point you may find yourself pondering how your daughter can remember every word to the latest Taylor Swift song but can't remember a simple thing like not sneezing directly into your face. Especially since that typically transpires when you've just opened your mouth to say something. Not that it matters because, despite the fact she's visibly oozing cold or flu-related funk, she's so damn sweet you'll inevitably be all up in her face giving good-night kisses anyway.

When it comes to our kids, love and affection take precedence over self-preservation, so you might as well resign yourself to becoming a living, breathing petri dish.

2. Teach your toddler to wash his hands frequently. Frequent hand washing is a necessity for you *and* your child. It's as important to your well-being as food, water, and possibly chocolate. Kids don't need to lick toilets to effectively spread germs; they do that by simply existing. My girls complain about having to wash their hands after each trip to the potty and before every meal, but that's one of those hard-and-fast rules I won't back down from. Someday, when they truly understand the nature of bacteria, they'll appreciate what didn't wind up in the green bean casserole thanks to my interference. Let the gagging and retching commence.

3. Teach your toddler to wipe his nose. But good luck with that. If you're lucky, you might convince your kid to properly use Kleenex before he's of legal drinking age, but until then be on the lookout for stray boogers. Picking one's nose is a rite of passage.

One night when she was three, Gray and I were cuddling in "Mommy and Daddy's big bed," as we often do. I told her a bedtime story, turned out the lights, and we snuggled in the dark. For a moment there was silence, and then, "Sorry for wiping boogers on your bed, Mom."

Talk about having to watch out for things that go bump in the night.

Splish splash, get your booty in the bath.

At some point during toddlerhood, your child will suddenly resist bath time like it's guerrilla warfare. If you're lucky, you'll face this demon while your kid is a toddler, because it's no picnic trying to come up with effective ways to convince a teenage boy to shave, bathe, break out the Axe body spray, and quit wearing two-day-old boxers. If a toddler fights back, you can generally woo him with bath crayons and floating alphabet letters. A teenager? Not so much.

I quickly discovered the best way to avoid nightly contention over getting clean. I load the tub with so many water-friendly distractions it looks like I've robbed an aquarium gift shop. We have a whole bathroom shelf dedicated to novelties such as rubber duckies, wind-up fish, rainbow-colored bubble bath, and nontoxic paints—everything short of seaweed and scuba gear—to convince my girls that getting clean is a *good* thing. Sometimes I even let them put on their swimsuits and pretend they're going to the beach. I do, however, draw the line at importing sand and renting a wave machine. You might be thinking, *This woman needs to tell her kids to suck it up and get in the damn tub.* And I say that sometimes too—in slightly less abrasive vernacular. But I'm all about trying to make bath time fun, and it seems to be working. Most days my girls go to preschool without dirty fingernails and crusty sweet potatoes in their hair. Please note I said *most* days.

The caveat with having scads of toys in the bathtub is they put a serious damper on your own showering experience. When I finally have a moment of peace to wash my hair—to let the hot water work some stress out of my shoulders and have my very own *Calgon, take me away* moment—I inevitably trip over a plastic octopus, stub my toe on a minisubmarine, or slip on a water squirting replica of Rome's Trevi fountain. But when you're desperate to have five minutes by yourself in the tub, the *last* thing you want to do is spend the first half of it picking up errant toys. I choose my battles, and you will too.

As a side note, music can be a huge help with buttering up your kids during bath time. Also, there's nothing cuter than watching a two-year-old attempt water ballet to the *Despicable Me* sound track while her hair is shampooed into a fauxhawk! When Gray was a baby, I made an iPod playlist of kid-appropriate, water-related songs, such as "Little April Showers" from *Bambi*, the infamous rubber ducky song from *Sesame Street*, and "Under the Sea" (if you don't know that's from *The Little Mermaid*, you clearly don't have daughters). We fondly refer to the playlist as *Gray's Bath Time Jam*, and it was a staple for a long time. In fact, it was a lovely accompaniment until Raffi's "Baby Beluga" got stuck in my head for three nights and I had vivid dreams of drowning our iPod in the toilet, right before peeing on it for good measure. That's when I decided we needed a little distance from our spa symphony.

Get creative with your tub-time entertainment. When you can pass off soaping and scrubbing as recreation, that's some admirable parenting chutzpah!

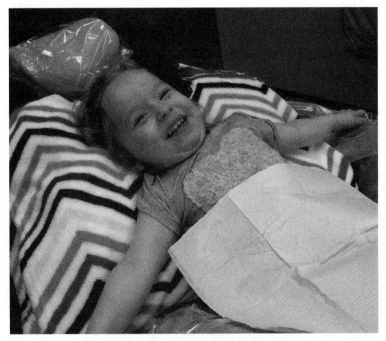

Gray is all smiles after her first dental exam. Mostly because they've just told her she's getting a free toothbrush. *Photo courtesy of Jenna von Oy.*

Don't get stuck in brush hour.

When your child is around two or three years old, you'll head to the dentist's office for a routine checkup of your own and your dentist will mention it's time to bring little Johnny in for his introduction to the wonderful world of dentistry. You'll nod in mock agreement, as your brain scrambles to remember how many times your kid has eaten sugar this week. Also, whether or not he remembers what flossing is in case there's a pop quiz. You'll spend the car ride home calculating the ratio of days your child has been on this planet relative to how many teeth he has and how many times you've bothered to legitimately brush them. By the time you pull into your driveway, you'll need a stiff drink, which sort of defeats the purpose of that cleaning you just had. Not that I'm trying to deter you from a cocktail.

Gray was so gleeful in advance of her first dentist visit you'd have thought we were carnival-bound. I didn't have the heart to tell her it was going to be the antithesis of candy apples and carousels and would likely go downhill from there. Why spoil the innocent excitement? After all, what's *not* thrilling about endless talk of magnificent molars and wonderful wisdom teeth? My daughter surprised the hell out of me by quietly sitting through the entire cleaning. She squirmed less than *I* normally do. Though I suppose that's not hard.

Once it was over, she thanked the dental technician, flashed her supersparkly pearly whites, and politely asked, "May I get a Rapunzel toothbrush now, Mommy?"

Aha! I knew there had to be a catch to the whole *sitting quietly and still* thing. Apparently she'd come up with a reward system I knew nothing about. Whatever happened to being bribed with something simple like Goldfish or a *Zootopia* sticker?

Rewards aren't necessarily a bad thing. Getting your kid serious about brushing his teeth isn't always smooth sailing. Sometimes teaching him not to eat the toothpaste or gnaw on his brush like it's a baby back rib is as far-fetched as convincing your husband to put the toilet seat down after a restroom trip. But that's okay! You have to start somewhere. I firmly believe it's worth letting your child nibble, lick, chew, gum, or suck on a few bristles if it means he gets accustomed to the routine of cleaning his teeth twice a day. Eventually he'll get the hang of it, and it'll no longer look like he's trying to stab his tongue with a Crest-coated plastic sword in lieu of actually removing plaque.

As with bath time, it's significantly easier to persuade children to brush if you can trick them into thinking it's a game. Thankfully, you have an arsenal of ideas to try out, including supportive books such as *The Tooth Book* by Dr. Seuss, and *Smile Spotters,* which also provides you with an Elf on a Shelf–like dental hygiene assistant in the form of a tooth fairy helper.

For a creative approach that doesn't involve purchasing anything, my sister-in-law used to "search for elephants" in her son's mouth to encourage him to open wide enough to reach his back teeth. I thought it was genius, and I altered the idea to fit Gray's inclinations. She was more enthralled with attempts to locate Alice in Wonderland and the Mad Hatter at the tea party in her mouth. That sounds like it might scar a child forever, but kids don't think about it like it's a tale from the dark side. All they hear is "Ooh, I see Snow White hiding behind a bicuspid!"

There are also game options if you purchase an Oral B Disney character toothbrush and download the free Magic Timer app that goes along with it. This thing single-handedly bamboozled my daughter into thinking she enjoyed brushing. And by *enjoyed*, I mean she begged me to let her do it several times a day. *Begged me! To brush her teeth!* How bananas is that? With this app, each time your child brushes, she'll uncover a still photo from the Disney movie that corresponds with the character on her brush. The photo then gets stored in a virtual sticker book she can flip through to admire her spoils whenever she wishes. Would you like me to let you in on the best part? It hypnotizes your kid into standing still for a full two minutes while brushing, the side benefits of which are unparalleled. That means you get *two full minutes* to sip a cup of coffee or take a pee break. And as we all know, sometimes motherhood is defined by prolonged periods of time when we desperately have to pee and can't. Your kid's teeth may not wind up expertly brushed, but . . . who cares? I'm not looking to sell you the Disney Kool-Aid, but who doesn't look forward to two minutes of peace and quiet? Can I get an amen?

Ar-"rest"-ed development.

Toddlers don't enjoy feeling like they're missing out on anything, so don't be surprised if your child starts refusing naptime . . . which is scarier than negotiating the rim of the Grand Canyon on roller skates.

A few weeks after Gray turned three, she informed me she no longer needed daily naps. She said she was happy to sleep during naptime at preschool, while her friends were doing the same, but she no longer required afternoon rest at home. Good thing three-year-olds have such a handle on their own needs.

I would've laughed in her face and sent her to bed faster than you can say *tough shit,* if it weren't for the fact she'd recently woken up in an immoderately foul mood every time she napped at home. Every. Single. Time. She was downright bearlike. And we're not talking Yogi & Boo Boo, cute-little-roly-poly-cub frolicking in the Yellowstone wilderness; we're talking monstrous grizzly ripping the roof off your hatchback to get at your picnic lunch. I'd begun to dread her naps more than doing my taxes. Which, technically speaking, I have someone *else* do because I hate them so much. Consequently, I thought she might be onto something—or at least that was my secret longing.

Believe it or not, every now and then a three-year-old presents a problem as well as its solution!

At her next pediatrician well visit, I inquired about the importance of maintaining a daily sleep schedule. I explained our ongoing battle with the postnap *nasties*.

"Naps are certainly still important," our awesome pediatrician told me, "but is she sleeping at school?"

"Like they've been spiking her snack-time milk with Benadryl," I responded. "Not to mention, she's also averaging ten hours a night."

"Well, as long as she's getting enough nightly rest and sleeping at school a few days a week," she told me, "I wouldn't worry about it."

Music to this mama's ears.

Obviously, solid sleep is a must for any toddler. As children get older, they graduate from the need for multiple naps per day to only one, and eventually that number dwindles to none. This pretty much sucks, because *you'll* have gotten used to the downtime too. Triple that if you reserve that hour or two for your personal me-time, and now your only privacy happens when you can score three minutes on the toilet. So enforce those siestas as long as you possibly can, and talk to your trusted pediatrician before you dispose of naptime.

Food for thought.

As a parent, I've found healthy meals get tougher and tougher to put on the table. Schedules are hectic and harried, everyone has a different agenda regarding what they will and won't eat, and trips to the farmer's market for fresh produce are fewer and farther between. Trips like that take time, and time isn't our own anymore.

When I was first married, I looked forward to the quiet evenings that inspired me to whip up a three-course meal. (*Quiet* being the key word there.) I view homemade meals as an extension of love, and I treasured the chance to share that with my husband. I would light candles, pour a glass of vino, turn on some music, and get to passionately mincing and dicing. I was a disciple of the kitchen, and I was truly in my element when I had an hour of uninterrupted cooking therapy.

Those days are long gone. While I still adore creating special, love-filled dishes for my husband, and now my kids too, I can barely lift my knife to chop a garlic clove before the tiny humans are calling for me to kiss a boo-boo, hoist them up, host a kitchen dance party, rescue a Hello Kitty doll from dog thievery, or make the predinner snack they insist on having because "I'm hungry right *now*, Mommy, and I can't wait five more minutes for the dinner you're making because that's going to take *forever!*" For the full visual, that line is delivered in the whiniest, highest-pitched, Minnie Mouse–like, most grating, three-going-on-thirteen voice you can possibly imagine. When I'm *really* having a night to remember, my dogs are also howling incessantly and the phone won't quit ringing. It's a laugh a minute.

Despite my current need to prep an entire meal before my daughters lose interest in whatever distraction I've drummed up for them, or break out into a scuffle over who technically owns the be-dazzled, glow-in-the-dark magic wand (which my wallet has its own opinion on), my biggest issue tends to be getting my girls to sit still and *actually* consume the meal I've put in front of them. Our dinner table is the battle frontline.

Here are a few things to take into consideration when refereeing the Kids versus Healthy Food altercation.

1. Kids can be pickier than a wedgie. It's exasperating when you've dodged toys and tantrums to put together a well-balanced meal, only to have your kid turn up her nose like you're serving pickled herring. Sometimes the only "delicacy" my children will commit to is mac 'n' cheese, which probably has Julia Child rolling over in her grave. I had a childhood friend who refused to eat anything except cheese pizza, hamburgers, and lettuce with sugar sprinkled on it. (Nutritionists across America just choked on their kale and quinoa salads.)

Thankfully, I have girls who love food almost as much as I do and who don't often turn down trying something new. But that doesn't mean I don't run into conflict every now and then. Sometimes toddlers use their newfound independence to reject the carrots and beg for tater tots instead. I'm certainly not suggesting you give in or rush off to fulfill their every whim—Lord knows how many times I've had to put my foot down and remind my kids I'm their mom, not their personal chef. Sometimes they even believe me! Right after they remind me I'm also their personal assistant, chauffeur, and housekeeper.

2. Sugar is a sneaky bastard. If I have trouble passing up *macarons* and salted caramel squares on any given day, I can only imagine how tough it is for my kids, who can't yet reconcile why roasted cauliflower is healthier than chocolate chip cookies. Especially when one so clearly tastes better than the other! My kids would be ecstatic if I suddenly told them we were having peanut butter parfait with a side of cream puffs for dinner, but that'll happen when I start my side career as a phone sex operator. Which is never, I pinky swear.

Unfortunately, sugar doesn't announce itself quite as blatantly when it's in other, more acceptable "dinner-friendly" items. Ketchup, store-bought spaghetti sauce, barbecue sauce, yogurt, and juice can all be guilty of high sugar content. Before you get to thinking I'm on my high horse, I'm not going to sit here and say I don't put them on the table from time to time anyway. Sometimes leaving sweets off the menu is harder than I want it to be. But since I don't want to deny my child every time she asks for a small after-dinner treat, I try to be mindful about how much sugar our main meals contain.

I also try to keep from stockpiling sweets in our pantry, but I mostly fail miserably at it. People seem to love showering us in confections, so we always wind up with more in the house than we should. Maybe folks take one look at my wonderfully plump, womanly thighs and think, *I bet she won't turn down a pastry.* And they'd be right; I have the willpower of a Burmese python. Even better, I'm a hypocritical dessert eater. I'm notorious for telling my kids "absolutely no dessert tonight," while stealthily inhaling a butterscotch brownie behind their backs. But I figure that's my prerogative as a parent and my reward for putting up with toddler drama.

3. Kids are sugar narcs. They can sniff out candy like a hound on the trail of a rib eye. So don't sneak a Butterfinger from their Halloween candy bucket unless you want to be called out on it! Double-bag all PMS-related chocolate stashes, and keep them on a high shelf behind the dusty wedding china. Hide that shit like you're sneaking French cheese through customs, then dispose of the wrappers in your neighbor's trash bin for an added layer of protection. But don't be surprised if your kid inspects your breath and figures you out anyway! Kids are clueless when you need five minutes to finish an important phone call (even though you're in midconversation, frantically mouthing, "I'm on the phone!"), but they can definitely tell when you've been pilfering candy. It's a gift.

4. Frequent snacking isn't convenient, but neither are hunger meltdowns. My kids always need a snack at the most inopportune times, such as when we're running late or I'm finally sitting down for the first time in seven hours. It drives me bonkers to fix a million minimeals a day, but I consider it a preemptive strike—it's imperative to keep my girls from getting overly hungry! In order to avoid having them turn into a couple of crankypants (if they were adults, I would have a far more creative name for it), I try to keep a roster of quick, healthy options available so my girls can graze. It stifles rumbling tummies without spoiling dinner! It also cuts down on extreme mood swings and gives my daughters the productive energy needed to haul out every toy they own, scatter them haphazardly under my feet, and then run circles around me while I slowly slip into the hypnotic haze of exhaustion. And who wouldn't want that?

5. Pizza delivery is hard to avoid unless you do some advanced food preparation. I'll plead the fifth on this one, but let's just say there's a reason I know it to be fact. I find we resort to less take-out when I think ahead. Whenever possible, I try to make a few large portions over the weekends so I have some built-in meals to rely on during the week. This way, when time gets away from me (which is every night), I'm not floundering for a quick fix. Because quick fixes tend to be heavy on the fat as well as the monthly budget!

6. It helps to keep a cache of simple, healthy go-to recipes on hand. When I'm at a loss for meal inspiration, I flip through my mental recipe book and pull out some tried-and-true recipes I know my girls love. If it ain't broke (or a healthy dish shrewdly camouflaged as a meal your kids actually enjoy eating), don't fix it!

7. Encourage exercise. And not just because you want your kid to pass out at the end of the evening, though that's a damn good incentive. It's beneficial to start getting your toddler primed for a nonsedentary lifestyle. If kids are encouraged to run, jump, dance, and climb trees when they're young, they're more likely to pass up the video games for a bike ride later on down the road. Or is that wishful thinking on my part?

Kids innately have more energy than a kangaroo chugging Red Bull. It probably goes without saying, but if they don't work off the energy from the food they're consuming, they'll never sleep. And if they never sleep, neither will you. End of story.

The internal food feud.

The point of this chapter is to promote healthy living, but I think it's also important to mention it's okay to improvise! Some nights I belatedly discover I've forgotten to defrost the chicken breasts I planned on grilling, and the only backup plan that doesn't involve take-out is dragging two kids to the grocery store. (Which would be so time-consuming—not to mention, sanity-defying—it wouldn't allow everyone to get to bed on time.) But that's fine, because you know what? It isn't detrimental to our kids' long-term health if we feed them cereal and milk for dinner once in a while! They can survive a meal that wouldn't win the *MasterChef* competition and/or doesn't perfectly reflect the five major food groups.

You know what else? Skipping a meal here and there won't kill our kids' brain cells or turn them toward lives of crime. It isn't inhumane to serve something unconventional every now and again, such as cold pizza for breakfast, and it's important to let yourself off the hook when you do! She writes as she simultaneously enrolls in the witness protection program to avoid backlash from the conservative child nutritional advocates out there . . .

THE MORAL OF MY STORY

I'm all for good hygiene and balanced meals, but I'm also a huge proponent of maintaining my *mental* balance. Sometimes I'm lucky to get my girls to eat more than one bite of pasta during dinner, and some nights they go to bed without bathing or brushing their teeth (oh, the shame!). Hell, some nights I'm lucky if *I* have an opportunity to bathe or brush my teeth before bed.

The bottom line? If you're up against a wall, don't bang your head against it. As long as you're making every possible effort to be a positive influence on your child's health practices, you're doing the right thing!

Gray discovers it's a great big world out there. At the
Children's Museum of Manhattan. *Photo courtesy of Jenna von Oy.*

CHAPTER 9

The Age of No Innocence

A SCENIC VIEW OF MY PAST

Once upon a really strange and exciting time of my life, people actually paid me to do cool, crazy things like fly on a trapeze for *Circus of the Stars*, sing the national anthem at NBA basketball games, and make out with Mark-Paul Gosselaar in the backseat of a car. In case you're wondering, the latter occurred during one particularly hot and steamy installment of the NBC Monday-night lineup. In a future episode of *This Is Your Life*, I hope they resurrect that footage to mock my miserable attempts at a sexy make-out session. Anyway, during that decade of (well-compensated and highly public) absurdity, the *Blossom* cast was also sent to France to film a special two-part miniseries called *Blossom in Paris*. This put the *oh là là* in my step like I'd been given free passes to a Chippendales convention with a pocketful of one dollar bills.

I'd been studying French for years in school, so I jumped at the chance to practice my skills, feast on baguettes and stinky cheese, and smirk back at the Mona Lisa. I couldn't wait to write postcards at quaint cafés in Montmartre, dance the night away at Gauloises-filled discotheques, and kiss every Jacques and Jean-Luc I set my eyes on. In a nutshell, I wanted to smooch and sightsee my way through the City of Love and Lights.

As luck would have it, I didn't do as much smooching as I'd

hoped for. But boy, did I ever sightsee! And the kind of "sightseeing" I'm referring to made a bigger impact on my carnal knowledge than any French kiss ever could have.

I wound up filming for only two days of my two-week "work" trip to Paris, so I spent the rest of it exploring. Since I was a minor, the production company had flown my mom and tutor along as my travel companions . . . otherwise known as *glorified chaperones*. But being underage and having an entourage didn't thwart my fun. How could it? Did I mention they were *paying* me to have a vacation? You can't beat getting per diem to mosey beneath the Eiffel Tower or peruse the Louvre Museum. I won't pretend I didn't welcome the perks with open arms. I also won't pretend I don't miss perks such as those, now that they're fewer and further between. I was one lucky little shit! At this very moment, I'd give my right arm to be strolling the Champs-Elysées and shoving crêpes down my throat on some-one else's euro. I'm even old enough to legally drink the wine now, dammit. Though, to be fair, I never really let that stop me.

But back to my point.

My mom and tutor and I spent our days learning *l'histoire de Paris*, while our nights were spent . . . hitting the hay before most Europeans had even put dinner on the table. Yes, my evenings saw me going to bed so early you'd have thought I was channeling one of the Golden Girls. Or that someone had slipped me an Ambien. Or both.

Alas, I was only sixteen, so the wild Paris nightlife wasn't in the cards for me. *C'est la vie*. Or perhaps more appropriately, *mèrde*! Sadly, most of my daylight adventures involved being stalked by dirty old men. Not really my idea of fun. As it turns out, my ability to charm young French studs was less than successful. I didn't even make it to the minor leagues. Instead, I drew in those silver-haired French foxes like a Venus flytrap. Go figure.

I guess I couldn't disguise my naive, all-American, girl-next-door vibe. It emanated like some sort of warped, jailbait pheromone, and apparently older French dudes dig that. Just ask Lolita.

I could tell you funny (creepy) stories about the guy who followed me into the ladies' room and tried to lock us in there together or about the hunchbacked grandpa who surprised his caretaker by abruptly turning his walker around to follow me in the opposite direction of the sidewalk. (For the record, I've never seen a ninety-year-old move that fast!) But the real kicker was the motorcycle cop who stopped at a traffic light and exposed himself as I walked by. Yes, my first view of a penis was during a drive-by masturbation from one of Paris's finest . . . in front of my mother and studio teacher.

On a scale of comfortable to excruciatingly, appallingly *un*comfortable, that incident actually ran off the scale and crash-landed on the other side. It wasn't quite the French lesson I was hoping for.

CUT TO . . .

If I thought my unintended ogling of Officer Dick at the age of sixteen was shocking, it's nothing relative to the things I find myself worrying I'll have to protect my own children from. Do you think I can get away with locking them in a soundproof, media-proof chamber until they turn eighteen?

Obviously, I'm kidding. I'll be locking them up until they're *at least* thirty-five.

MY CRADLE CHRONICLES

Someday, when I write the twenty-third sequel to this book, titled *Situation Grandmomedy*, we can really delve into the depth and breadth of my neuroses regarding the terrifying world in which we're raising our children. Then again, I don't need to spell out all of the scary scenarios for you, do I? They already weigh heavily upon you because you're a mom too. You're already losing sleep over the same things I am, because we're both on an eternal quest to keep our children safe from harm.

I don't want to toss more logs of fear onto your already blazing inferno, but leading our children into toddlerhood means we're also opening up their world to all sorts of new interactions and circumstances. Some will be stunningly beautiful and positive; others will be the exact opposite. With that in mind, I think it warrants a discussion on some of the evils that might lurk in the shadows.

Who's afraid of the big, bad wolf?

From the moment we learn we've conceived a child, we turn ourselves over to a life of worry. We spend our first trimester nervous we'll eat the wrong cheese or forget to take our prenatal pills. We fret over whether or not crib bumpers are dangerous and tear our hair out trying to decide if our newborn's crying indicates something worse than a dirty diaper or hunger. We agonize about tripping over tiny toes, pinching sweet little fingers in drawers, and improperly babyproofing. When they learn to walk, we sweat every sharp table corner, steep staircase, and moving car.

As our children grow, so grows our unease. We realize the bigger their comfort zone gets, the harder it is to keep them safe in it. And at the end of the day, that's our want—scratch that, our most intense parental *need*—to keep our children safe, secure, and healthy. Beyond our desire they'll find the love of their lives, gift us with grandbabies, achieve career success and financial security, find inner peace and happiness, inspire those around them, and lead confident, faithful lives filled with honesty, integrity, and loyalty, we pray for their health and protection. Guarding them is our lifework.

Worrying comes with the parenting territory. The truth of the matter is, we live in a world filled with hatred, racism, sexism, and every social injustice you can think of. I don't know what it will take to get us out of this paralyzing mess we're in. There's too much access to information, weapons, drugs, and intolerance and not enough access to empathy, therapy, understanding, and mutual respect. It can get deeply depressing, and it's hard not to have a heavy heart regarding the current state of humanity. But it's also imperative we maintain our belief in the inherent goodness of one another. Nothing magnifies the need to embrace kindness and goodwill more than being a parent.

To place too much focus on the negative events and conditions around us is to promote paranoia and living in constant fear. That doesn't help our children *or* our parenting. By the same token, not giving enough attention to those negative events and conditions— choosing to pretend they don't exist—can be equally devastating. Because part of shaping our children is preparing them for the reality of the world we live in. It's a very delicate, challenging, thought-provoking balance.

It would be hypocritical for me to suggest you shouldn't feel troubled, or even paranoid, over how to best protect your kids. I haven't mastered that either. Hell, I can't even keep my girls from catching a stomach virus at day care; how can I ignore the looming fears about more disturbing horrors? I'll spend the rest of my life earning the unavoidable gray hair and wrinkles, because I know what a great big, unpredictable world it is out there. Sometimes there really *are* monsters under the bed, even though I tell my kids it's only dust bunnies and a pair of old sneakers.

You'll notice somewhat of a joke deficit in this portion of the chapter, and I do mean we're about to abruptly jump off the comedy cliff. That's on purpose. Beneath my layer of shallow sarcasm is the true soul of my motherhood, and I just can't find the funny in dark subjects such as peer pressure, drug and alcohol abuse, suicide, body shaming, sexual promiscuity, or stranger danger. Nor do I want to. Those are some of the things that haunt me. They aren't just my nightmares; they're my daymares. They're the dragons I hope I can slay for my children and pray I never need to. At the risk of coming across as a cynical, paranoid, overprotective, neurotic mom (I'd rather be honest than up my mommy street cred), I can't imagine writing this chapter without opening up about some of my personal anxieties and broaching a few very unfunny and unglamorous subjects.

We have a few years before some of these issues will enter the picture (with any luck, most of them *never* will), but I think it's helpful to acknowledge and address them now. In a sense, we never stop being afraid of the dark. With that in mind, I hope to shed some light on a few of the challenges of toddlerhood safety.

As a side note—if you're looking to remain blissfully ignorant in your motherhood endeavors, this is probably a good time to skip to the next chapter.

The World Wide Web of Deceit

In this age of ever-growing technology, accessibility is one of the biggest enemies we parents face. It has become our Achilles' heel, only Achilles never had to worry about devastating horrors such as terrorist attacks or school shootings. Innocence isn't a lengthy visitor these days, thanks to the Internet, television, video games, and social media. To a certain extent, we're being forced into earlier conversations about everything from losing one's virginity, to the world at war, to the topic of being transgender. Because if *we* don't talk to our kids about important, relevant issues, rest assured someone else will. I believe some of these conversations need to begin during toddlerhood.

To put this in perspective, I'm not suggesting you engage your four-year-old in a dialogue about every evil in existence. I'm happy to say my girls don't yet know the first thing about what words such as *genocide* or *suicide bombings* mean. They probably can't even pronounce them. The closest my kids come to understanding the concept of evil stems from a five-minute discussion we recently had about which Disney witch is the cruelest. (According to Gray, it's a toss-up between Ursula from *The Little Mermaid* and Maleficent from *Sleeping Beauty*.)

I'd like to maintain my kids' innocence as long as possible, so I don't turn on the news for background noise or discuss world events with my husband in their presence. I am, however, keenly aware they're absorbing minor fragments of news-related information anyway. Our nation is obsessed with hopping on its unfiltered political soapbox, so completely sheltering our kids is wishful thinking. Unless you live on your own island somewhere, with no cable, Internet, newspapers, or guests. Then I suppose you're off the hook. As well as, I imagine, bored off your ass.

It's nearly impossible to completely avoid exposure to current events, particularly since toddlers soak up more than we give them credit for. They hear teachers and other adults in passing and catch snippets as you change the channel over to *Curious George*. Someday those bits and pieces will start forming a more comprehensive picture, and a basic understanding will begin to take shape. I dread that day. Until it arrives, I'll keep encouraging lists for Santa Claus, praising the magic of make-believe, sprinkling pretend fairy dust, and hoping beyond hope I can keep my girls from being as corrupted as I am.

Wish me luck.

Despite my affinity for surfing the web, perusing news feeds, and posting lengthy blog posts about my zany motherhood anecdotes, here are a few of the chief pitfalls of the Internet, as I see them.

1. The Internet is deceiving. It makes things look good. Reeeeally good. Cindy Crawford good. George and Amal Clooney sunbathing in the nude in St. Tropez good.

It glamorizes everything from dieting to sexting to stalking to substance abuse to guns . . . which is terrifying, socially irresponsible, and dangerous. My point? The Internet throws glitter and glamor at frightening subjects and makes them razzle-dazzle like a Fourth of July fireworks finale. Which makes our parenting job that much tougher.

2. Once information is out there, it's nearly impossible to take it back again. In other words, don't post those pictures of your two-year-old sitting on the toilet for the first time, if you think it might come back to haunt him later. And it will, I promise!

The Internet is a peculiar beast—it lets photos and information take on a life of their own . . . explains the girl who would love to get rid of those half-naked photos of herself in a bikini from that charity fashion show years ago, when she didn't realize paparazzi had been granted front-row access. Oops. Here's hoping my own stupidity saves you from yours.

3. Even strictly monitored computer access isn't foolproof. Parenting has never been harder, because it's not easy to regulate what your kids are privy to. I don't know about you, but I'll be damned if my girls stumble upon the definition for "Eiffel Towering" someday while innocently looking up monuments in Paris. If you're feverishly researching that term right now, I sympathize. I had no clue what it meant until they mentioned it on an episode of *Scandal*. Right after I asked my husband if *he* knew what it was (he didn't), I consulted

Urban Dictionary. I'm not what one would call *conservative*, but the answer made even *me* blush!

Despite attentive administration control over your home electronics, access to for-adult-eyes-only material can potentially weasel its way in. Sadly, young children aren't totally out of the woods. I'm not saying your toddler will find a way to sneak in a Saturday matinee of *Debbie Does Dallas* (at least you'd better hope not!), but your line of defense may not be entirely impervious either. One minute your little girl is watching scenes from *Frozen* on Kids YouTube, the next minute she's watching some creepy-ass guy dressed in an Elsa costume, singing in front of anatomically correct snowmen. Ew. Just nasty. (And how the hell did *that* make it past my strict parental controls?)

Even if your kid isn't online at all and/or you have complete control over what your own kids view, you can't control what their friends watch at home or talk about at school. And toddlers can't always discern what constitutes an appropriate discussion. Hell, they still don't know not to fart in front of company. The only advice I can offer is, don't don those parenting blinders under the guise of having a child that's "too young to worry about." Keep your computer on lockdown, make sure you have family-friendly restrictions set, and monitor usage as closely as possible. Beyond that, prepare yourself for a few discussions you aren't yet ready for, such as "Mommy, what is twerking?" (Wince.)

Not exactly my idea of a Hallmark moment.

4. The Internet will put crazy words in your kid's mouth faster than you can say "ridonculous." Potty training takes months to master. Meanwhile, your toddler manages to adopt the word *stupid* as his favorite adjective in under twenty seconds.

5. The Internet is just the beginning of the addiction. If you're anything like me, your toddler has *extremely* limited access to the Internet or any number of products that open the door and beckon him into cyberspace. But toddlers eventually turn into teenagers, and your child's use of electronics isn't going to disappear anytime soon.

As I mentioned earlier, one day (possibly next week) you'll wake up to find your child knows the inner workings of your laptop better than you do. And your iPad. And your cell phone. We live in the digital age, so there's no use in fighting it. Your kid will use electronics to further his education in school and then come home to ignore his homework in lieu of playing some weird game based on car thievery, the redeeming qualities of which have you thoroughly stumped. If you're *extra* lucky, he'll camp out in front of his video console until you're dragging him away like a sack of potatoes. A bellowing, braying, leave-you-wishing-for-the-good-old-days-when-he-still-wanted-to-climb-trees-and-catch-frogs sack of potatoes. I'm not sure they make emojis to cover that scenario.

Right now we're in the super-early stages of the electronics obsession, when we can embrace some control and sanity. Since that won't last forever, let's take it where we can get it, shall we?

Social security administration

These days, people get their kicks from posting about everything they do. And I do mean *everything*. If you're anything like me, you've unfollowed a Facebook friend or two because they've worn you out with never-ending offensive political rants, raunchy drunk photos, cuss-filled posts, or annoying pyramid schemes. I love freedom of speech as much as the next person, but there are people out there who seem to get off on crossing the line and then turning around to stomp on it like a cigarette butt! I can only take so much.

I'm all for tweeting and blogging and posting. Sharing is caring, right? But I try to make thoughtful decisions about what I put out there for everyone else's consumption and input. I draw the line at letting folks know when I'm headed to the gynecologist for a pap smear, for instance, or when my husband and I are squeezing in a romp.

I believe some activities are simply meant to be kept private. And you know what? Your privacy comfort level might be on the opposite end of the spectrum from my own. You might think I overshare too, and that's okay! I thoroughly respect that. We all have different boundaries, and it's good when we can recognize them. I'm confident you know when to take a break from reading my blogs, close my book, or turn off one of my television interviews. My real concern is oversharing as it pertains to our kids.

We live in a society where teenagers are vlogging about their personal lives and dropping pins so the whole world can identify their geographic location. iPhones are being turned into built-in tracking devices. Who needs a LoJack system when you have a smartphone, am I right? And while it might assist some parents in keeping tabs on their kids—apparently reading diaries is out and parental cyberstalking is in—it also opens the door for others to do the same. It's scary as hell.

Kids can be gullible, and predators are out there. I hope giving my daughters an early introduction to personal safety, as well as continual clear dialogue about stranger danger, will give way to better and more cautious choices down the road. It's never too early to start teaching your children to protect themselves!

Bullying

When I was a kid, the bullies were known schoolwide. They were the rough-and-tumble guys who wore motorcycle jackets and pushed nerds into lockers before the morning bell rang or stole lunch money from cubbies when no one was looking. They might as well have worn giant sandwich boards with threats like, *Don't mess with me or I'll date your sister!* If one wanted to avoid them, all one had to do was feign a fever during recess or bypass dodgeball at PE. These days, most bullies hide behind a cloak of invisibility called *their computer*, and cyberbullying is significantly harder to avoid.

Social media and the Internet have blown the door wide open for bullies to take out their own insecurities on the world at large. There's no shortage of people who prey on vulnerability, and there's no shortage of folks who are haunted by it. That goes for adults too. Lord knows I've dealt with my share of asshats who get off on tweeting malicious, perverse, horribly inappropriate things to me simply because they draw courage from that deceptive power called *anonymity*. No one is immune to bullying these days, no matter how thick his or her skin might be.

It may seem premature to bring the subject of bullying up while discussing toddlerhood, but it's alarming how early on it can rear its ugly head. Sadly, at some point our children might be stuck learning an unexpected lesson about it, and kids aren't as emotionally equipped for that as we are.

The foundation of bullying and peer pressure lies in what our children are taught from a young age. Toddlers are observers. They're in the throes of mental and physical development, so they spend their days watching and learning. They're influenced by *everything*—parents, siblings, teachers, classmates, strangers, books, television . . . You name it, they're paying attention to it. They collect thoughts and actions like a philatelist collects stamps, and then they whip them out when the situation calls for it. Or when it doesn't. Or simply when they feel like trying something on for size. You think your kid missed hearing the word *ass* in the middle of that pop song on the radio? No such luck. He has that filed away until he's ready to ask what it means or until he can find a creative way to work it into a conversation with the most conservative person you know.

Toddlerhood is also when our children really begin to understand and embrace empathy and compassion. It's when they realize actions and words have consequences, both good and bad. It's when they gain an understanding that hitting and pushing and shouting and pouting can be effective forms of communication, but so can hugging and helping and smiling and sharing. I imagine you're doing your darnedest to teach the beautiful benefits of positive gestures such as those. However, it isn't a foolproof way to prevent your child from encountering bullies. Because the fact is, not every other parent out there will set her child on the same path you do. Bullies have parents too.

I'm no medical or social expert (surprise!), so I'm not in a position to tell you how to handle any bullying that might come along. I'm essentially here for commiseration. That said, I believe we can all start by teaching our own kids the basics. Killing 'em with kindness is pretty dang effective! You never know—your child might be the light of kindness that leads someone else's child out of the bullying dark.

I want to raise feisty girls who recognize their own worth, but I don't want them to be inappropriately or disrespectfully feisty. There can be a fine line there, so my approach is ever-evolving. I can't offer infallible parenting, but the foundation of my efforts never changes. I'm going to keep reinforcing and encouraging kindness. I'm doing my best to build my daughters' self-esteem, while making sure they also learn the grace of humility. I'll continue teaching them to stand up for themselves, their convictions, and those around them who don't feel strong or comfortable enough to do the same. I'll provide a support system through every heartbreak, crisis, mental and physical hurt, and mistake they make, and I'll work hard to make sure they never feel alone. I'll teach my girls to wield the sword of self-confidence, and I'll do my best to parent them in an open, sincere, and unconditionally loving way that helps them respect their hearts and their bodies. We all have to start somewhere.

We may not be able to completely safeguard our children from the bullies out there, but we can teach them how to handle themselves in the face of one and how not to become one in the process. We can teach love above all else, and we do that by practicing what we preach.

Private parts and privacy

No parent enjoys opening the proverbial can of worms, but I believe honest discussions about your child's private parts and privacy can mean the difference between them opening up about being inappropriately touched (God forbid) or suffering in shame and silence. There comes a point when you realize it's time to introduce your toddler to some vocabulary words you hope he'll use sparingly. And not in front of anyone over the age of seventy.

What's in a name?

I'm in the Pretty Please Don't Use Cute Code Words for Your Child's Genitalia camp. I strongly support calling private parts by their anatomically correct names. Girls don't have a *tu-tu* or a *hoo-hoo* or any other word that sounds like it belongs in a Dr. Seuss rhyme or Shel Silverstein poem. It's a vagina. Similarly, boys don't have a *wee-wee* or a *winky*. They have a penis. I understand keeping adult concepts at bay and offering age-appropriate subjects, and I realize how crass it can be to hear the word *testicle* come out of your three-year-old's mouth (albeit hilarious, provided you aren't in line at the church fish fry). But proper language is crucial for development and a true understanding of what's going on with your child's body. Using accurate terms such as *breasts* and *bottom* helps to relay the notion there's nothing to feel ashamed of. Code words can sometimes make a child feel as if their body parts are bad.

Accurate terms also ensure your child can tell a teacher or trusted adult if something is wrong, uncomfortable, or painful. When a caregiver has to decipher what your kid means by "My noodle is bleeding," your son may not get medical attention as quickly as he should.

Your comfort level with these words and concepts will help dictate your child's comfort level too. If you turn redder than Marilyn Monroe's lipstick at the mere mention of anatomy, your kid will likely pick up on your embarrassment. We're adults now, people! It'd probably be good if we can get past that whole *pulling the shades down and giggling about reproduction* thing that began back in third grade. I know some parents find proper names to be too harsh or explicit for their little one, and I respect that. But may I suggest using the generic term *private parts* until you're ready to bust out the more specific language? For communication's sake, it's helpful if we can at least put the training wheels on the bike.

Naked lunch. And dinner. And everything in between.

Privacy tends to be elusive when it comes to toddlers. They aren't predisposed to keeping their pants on, so you might have your work cut out for you. By nature, toddlers are streakers, flashers, and exhibitionists. For example, they think nothing of removing articles of clothing in the middle of a birthday dinner for Grandma or streaking through your neighbor's yard hollering, "Look, Ma, no pants!" Little girls will lift their dresses in public, and little boys will touch themselves. It's all part of the deal. The trick is discreetly and subtly letting them know what is and isn't appropriate, without drawing so much attention that it makes them even more fixated than they already are.

The Early Bird Has Less Stress Down the Road

I believe it's never too early to introduce privacy and personal safety concepts such as closing the bathroom door or respecting one's own body. Since we can't follow our child's every move for all of eternity (a full-time job known as *impossible*), our responsibility is laying the groundwork. There's no need to dump every ounce of safety information on your kid like it's tires in a landfill; it's all about baby steps. The end game isn't to instill paranoia; it's to establish awareness—even in its simplest and mildest forms. Eventually you'll be broaching heavier subjects such as saying no to drugs, not getting into a car with strangers, and the difference between proper and improper touching. At the beginning, however, you'll likely be teaching easier lessons such as looking both ways before crossing the street and telling Mommy or Daddy if something feels uncomfortable. Every lesson is valuable, no matter how minor it seems . . . even if it simply revolves around teaching your toddler to trust his Spidey senses when they start tingling! So trust your *own* instincts, and pace yourself.

Gray and I stroll a beach in the Hamptons while visiting my *Celebrity Wife Swap*, Jill Zarin, in 2014. I was pregnant with Marlowe, and it was the first time Gray had seen the ocean. Her innocence and excitement were a sight to behold. *Photo courtesy of Jenna von Oy.*

Let Love Win

As a fellow mom, I don't know how to tell you to get past that daily underlying fear in your heart. There are, undoubtedly, some horrible and terrifying things out there. We have only to watch ten minutes of the nightly news before our stomachs churn with sadness and disgust over the state of affairs. And how can we "move beyond" it, when the sources of our fear aren't capable of being eradicated?

Some days my dread hides in the shadows; others it's more prominent. But being an ignorant mommy is impossible (not to mention potentially dangerous), so I make a conscious decision to push past the fear and anxiety.

The way I see it, all we can really do is combat adversity with even more love. In the darker moments, clouded with pessimism and despair, I try to remind myself that for every cowardly, vicious, selfish, evil person that exists out there, there are a thousand times as many brave, beautiful souls walking around, ready to help our children become the best adults they know how to be. The fight begins at home, and it's the only type of fighting I truly sanction. We have to arm our children with generosity, patience, humility, respect, tolerance, and a relentless love for one another. It's the most profound and long-lasting gift we can give them.

THE MORAL OF MY STORY

The second my children were out of the womb, I was struck with panic over the thought they might be safer back in it. I can't defend my girls from every negative influence or threatening situation they're met with in this lifetime, but it won't stop me from trying. I'll never be Supermom, but I hold the sincere hope that, despite my imperfections, I'll always be considered a hero in my daughters' eyes. I wish the same for you.

A picture is worth a thousand words. And a thousand laughs too.
Photo courtesy of Mimosa Arts.

CHAPTER 10
Sibling Rivalry Meets Sibling Revelry

A SCENIC VIEW OF MY PAST

For a short period of time during the *Blossom* years, my family and I rented an apartment next to the Warner Bros. Studio Ranch in Burbank, California. We were even there during the great Northridge quake of '94.

For a completely sidetracked side note, I was dating Will Friedle of *Boy Meets World* fame at the time. A few days before the earthquake, he'd given me a single red rose in a show of affection. Be still, my sappy little infatuated heart! I put that rose in a delicate glass vase in a position of high honor—the center of our dining room table. When the rattling began, in all its jarring, 6.7 glory, dishware crashed like NASCAR vehicles, art deco lamps shattered (which was probably for the better), and heavy IKEA furniture pieces swayed as if they were made of Jell-O. Guess what happened to my beloved rose? Despite being set in something so fragile, it was the only thing that remained upright amidst the chaos and rubble. I took it as a clear sign of Will's eternal, undying love for me . . . We broke up not long after.

But back to the *real* story. This is the chapter my littlest brother will either hold against me forever or show his own children someday. Or both. (Sorry, not sorry, Tyler!)

Given that we were still trying to pull off a bicoastal residency in 1994, my dad spent the majority of his time in Connecticut with my two middle siblings. My parents had mutually decided this was the best route to go so my dad wouldn't lose his job and so the other kids could continue their education at the school we'd grown up in. Meanwhile, my mom stayed in Los Angeles with my youngest brother and me.

Without my dad around, my mother sometimes left Tyler in my care while running a quick errand to the bank or grocery store. And why shouldn't she? If I was old enough to drive a car, date boys, and have a full-time career, surely I could handle watching a six-year-old boy for a while, right?

Wrong.

Unbeknownst to my mother, Tyler's angelic face belied his devilish nature. Those Frank Sinatra blue eyes and cherubic cheeks (not to mention the naturally platinum hair Gwen Stefani would *kill* for) all added up to one adorable little wolf in sheep's clothing. Whenever my mom left me in charge, shit hit the fan like we were the main attraction in the chimp exhibit at the San Diego Zoo.

On several such occasions, my mom returned with her milk and eggs to find a screaming match that could've given a nest of pterodactyl babies a run for their money. Each time, I would passionately plead my case, referencing the Jekyll and Hyde act my brother seemed to be perfecting. But either I sucked at a decent defense strategy (I won't be gunning for Gloria Allred's job anytime soon) or my arguments were overshadowed by Tyler's impossible charm and adorability. Tyler's Cute Factor: 1. Jenna's Whiny Teenage Pleas: 0.

Rather than vindication, I was even chastised a time or two. "You're sixteen and he's only six, for God's sake," my mother would sputter. "You should be able to handle babysitting your own brother for thirty minutes. If you can't be mature and responsible enough for *that*, maybe you're not mature and responsible enough to handle going to the movies with your friends tonight either."

This prompted an angry, angst-ridden adolescent wail loud enough to drown out the traffic on the 405 freeway. And the Wild West stunt show at Universal Studios. And maybe even the sound of all the young Hollywood ingénues namedropping over cocktails at the Roxbury.

And so I set about getting even, enlisting the assistance of my other brother, who'd come out for a visit. Peter was no stranger to Tyler's antics or his uncanny ability to get away with them, so it didn't take much convincing. In no time, Pete was my conniving cohort in a devious little plan of entrapment. Now, entrapment may not be acceptable in police procedure—I learned this on *Law & Order*—but there are no rules when it comes to siblings. All's fair in revenge and retaliation.

The next time my mom left on an errand, Pete and I grabbed the cassette recorder (yes—I'm that old), popped in a tape, and pushed the button that would implicate that little cretin once and for all.

When my mom returned from shopping, she walked in on the usual catastrophic conditions. It looked like the Northridge quake had released the wrath of yet another aftershock. Toys were strewn about, tears were flowing (Pete's and mine), and we had Tyler locked in a coat closet. He was squealing like a stuck pig.

"What happened *this* time?" my mother demanded with exasperation as she hurried to free Tyler from his jail of winter jackets and rain boots.

"He took it a step too far," I complained.

"He went into your bedroom, locked himself in, and jammed sharp objects under the door at us," Peter added.

My mother looked at Tyler expectantly.

"They shoved me into the closet and locked me in there for no reason," he told her innocently. "I didn't do anything to them!" My mother's face started to soften, and Pete and I jumped on it before she completely caved.

"We have proof," I asserted as Pete pressed the incriminatory Play button.

My mom's face sagged as Tyler's shouting filled our tiny apartment. Even on that shoddy, muffled Walkman, it sounded like he'd been infiltrated by a poltergeist; I've heard horror film sound tracks that were less hair-raising. He's damn lucky we didn't have a video camera. Or YouTube.

Tyler's number was up. My mother confiscated his favorite toy, a hobbyhorse, and donated it to charity as punishment. Meanwhile, Pete and I breathed a sigh of relief and celebrated our victory.

My babysitting days were officially over.

CUT TO . . .

My babysitting days were *far* from over. In fact, they eventually turned into a full-time gig, made exponentially more frenzied when my husband and I decided Gray wasn't meant to be an only child. You think one kid is tough? Wait until you have the second one. You'll be working harder than Anthony Weiner's press rep.

Let the games begin.

MY CRADLE CHRONICLES

Bringing a new baby into your already hectic picture is nothing short of phenomenal. And brave. Milton Berle was once quoted as saying, "If evolution really works, how come mothers only have two hands?" Similarly, I mentioned in my first book that if God were a woman, mothers would be equipped with a self-cleaning option and built-in colostomy bag. The truth? Even if you had all of those things, it might not prepare you for juggling multiple children. In theory, one plus one equals two. In child rearing, one plus one equals all hell breaking loose. In other words, just when you think you've got a leg up on the whole parenting thing, your second kid will go and change all the rules. It's the best of times and the worst of times.

Houston, we have a pregnancy . . . again!

So you're having *another* baby! Yay! And *holy crap*! As if it weren't enough to put your body through nine-plus months of maternity mayhem on the first go round, you've decided to do it all over again. *Congratulations!* You're officially out of your ever-loving mind.

I say that with the utmost love and respect, of course.

Don't get me wrong: there's nothing easy about parenting a single child, but you're finally in a groove. You've started feeling settled. You know how to schedule according to the needs of a toddler and (mostly) balance your own responsibilities while still catering to the wacky whims of a tiny human. You've successfully found a way to work through your email backlog, keep your kid busy while you get a quiche in the oven, and even resurrect your sex life. Which is what got you into this mess.

Now you find yourself with a swollen belly, morning sickness (betcha really missed *that*, huh?), a resurgence of baby brain, and the need to track down every pregnancy book you've loaned out to friends. Just because you've been through it before doesn't mean you remember *how* you got through it!

As soon as you're past the initial excitement over the prospect of bringing home a new addition, your toddler will shock you back into the reality that you're about to be ringmaster of your very own three-ring circus. The wistful, slow-motion montage of baby coos, early morning feedings, and itty-bitty bloomers will be shattered by your four-year-old running full monty through the house shrieking, "I'm never wearing pants to school again! You can't *make* me!"

The upside? Chasing after a toddler will help your pregnancy go by faster than the Hogwarts Express.

A Ticking Time Mom

Every mom has moments when she struggles under the weight of dividing her time and affections—especially between children she loves more than life itself. Moms of multiple children have full-time attention deficit disorder; there's no rest for the weary! Actually, there's no rest in general. Rest is like an old friend you've had a falling out with.

Though Brad and I never questioned having more children, my brain pelted me with crazy questions during my second pregnancy such as, *What if you don't love this child as much as the first?* and *What if Gray is so irreversibly altered by having a sibling she doesn't become the woman she's meant to be?* and *How will you handle two kids when one makes you so tired you're borderline narcoleptic by lunchtime?* Thank God for close girlfriends who told me they'd asked the very same questions. It made me feel a hell of a lot less alone. Or insane.

Here are a few reminders that might make *you* feel less crazy and alone in the throes of it too.

1. Don't forget pregnancy and childbirth can put our systems in a bigger state of upheaval than the financial affairs of Greece. Emotions run high, compounded by inconsistent sleep and a toddler to chase after. Not to mention, your heart is busy making room to swell with even more love—as if that's possible! And I promise you, it is. It's not only okay to admit when you're feeling overwhelmed or apprehensive; it's healthy. I hope you have someone you feel comfortable confiding in—be it your partner, mom, best friend, therapist, or random Uber driver—so it helps take the edge off. You don't have to go it alone! Just because you've had a baby before doesn't mean you won't have concerns about labor and delivery or the change in lifestyle. This is one life experience that isn't like riding a bike. Sometimes we have to put our training wheels back on, even though we've already been around the block. Don't let anyone make you feel you should have all the answers simply because you aren't a first-time mom! There's always more to learn. Which is both wonderful and terrifying.

2. Don't be surprised if your concerns don't immediately disappear once the new baby is born. When I gave birth to Marlowe, my fears about finding more love for her receded like John Travolta's hairline. Love came out of the woodwork, and I suddenly understood the idea of loving one's children equally but differently. It was one of those concepts that didn't make sense until it was staring me in the face.

That doesn't mean all my anxieties went the way of the dinosaurs. I still fretted about being able to appropriately balance the needs of two kids, and I discovered I'd forgotten some of the Baby 101 I'd mastered when Gray was first born. I did my best to take a deep breath and rely on my mommy instincts.

3. Don't let a guilty conscience wear the pants. Take it from my eternally present Catholic guilt and me—it's all too easy to fall prey to feelings of inadequacy and remorse in the first days (or weeks, or months) of simultaneously parenting a toddler and a newborn.

I felt particularly bad during the first few weeks following Marlowe's birth via C-section. I was bummed about not being able to drive Gray to day care, cried over not being able to lift her due to doctor's orders, and mourned the inability to lie next to her in bed as she fell asleep due to concerns over tearing my stitches. Not being able to have her sit in my lap while I healed was devastating for both of us, especially considering I was allowed to hold and nurse the baby during that time. It hurt my heart. I knew my firstborn baby needed me too, and I couldn't give her as much of myself as I wanted. It probably comes as no surprise that Gray recovered more quickly from the situation than I did. She was overwhelmingly understanding. I was simply overwhelmed.

The emotional repercussions of giving birth for a second time affected me most when it came to dividing attention. It took time for me to wrap my head around the new normal. It's impossibly hard to feel like you have to "choose between children." Technically there's no choosing, of course, but it frequently feels like that nonetheless.

To effectively parent two children—or a whole brood, for that matter—you have to put the most urgent needs first. And when there's a newborn in the picture, they're generally promoted to priority. There were countless evenings when Marlowe needed me to feed her more than Gray needed me to put her to bed, but knowing that didn't make it any easier to hear Gray crying out for me. You can be the most attentive, levelheaded, confident, practiced parent on the planet, but it's hard to accept that you can't always be everything to everyone at all times.

All we can do is try our best and make sure everyone knows they're unconditionally loved. Giving love is never a parenting failure.

4. Don't forget to laugh. Some moments call for hyperventilating into a paper bag, while others call for a shot of hilarity. Still others call for a different kind of shot altogether, which is what they make those little airplane bottles for. I'll let you decide when it's appropriate to raid your liquor cabinet.

Speaking of airplane bottles . . . There are times when it's easy to inject humor into a strenuous situation, because you know there's a light at the end of the tunnel. Take one of the times I flew across the country with both of my daughters, for example.

They were three years and eight months old, respectively. As you may or may not know, traveling with children is the equivalent of purposely walking across hot coals, while juggling swords, while wearing a helmet full of live bees. But since I'm a glutton for punishment, I brought my girls along on a work trip.

After several flight delays and a desperate, not-at-all graceful attempt to drag two kids, two bags, and my sanity to the very back of the coach cabin, I was secretly praying for a Bloody Mary. And maybe a time machine so I could rethink my travel plans altogether. As soon as we took our seats, the flight attendant announced, "Ladies and gentlemen, please let me know if there's anything I can do to make your flight more comfortable."

I looked at Gray, who was hiccupping and crying from exhaustion (and also covered from head to toe in yogurt), and Marlowe, who was tearing at my blouse in search of the booby bar, and I called out, "Do you babysit?"

Like I said, sometimes the comedy just jumps out and whacks you in the face—your worn-out, hasn't-seen-sleep-in-days, didn't-have-time-for-makeup face.

But not all moments make it easy to unearth your inner comedienne . . . especially when you can't help one child without momentarily "neglecting" the other. I try to practice what I preach about laughing though my most challenging, frustrating mommy moments, but my sense of humor doesn't always prevail. I'm just making this whole mommy thing up as *I* go along too. You aren't the only one!

Kindling the Kinship

Since you already know the ins and outs of preparing yourself for the birth of your brand-new bundle of joy (unless baby brain has already disposed of all that information for you), let's jump to the preparations you might feel less certain about. Namely, how to convince your older child that a new brother or sister will be exciting in a way that doesn't completely muck up life as he knows it. Which, by the way, is *exactly* what's about to happen. The best you can hope for is managing to make introductions without the sky falling. Or at least without traumatizing both children in the process.

Ch-ch-ch-changes

Preparing your firstborn for a sibling requires one part planning, two parts ingenuity, oodles of love, and an unquantifiable amount of patience (though I suppose the word *crapload* might cover it).

Forethought is your friend. I recommend starting your sibling introduction preparation several months in advance. Don't wait until the ninth hour (or ninth month) to explain why your belly looks like you've swallowed a watermelon or why you're so emotional your tears are streaming more consistently than Pandora.

Kids don't always adjust well to change, so it's important to give them plenty of time to grow accustomed to schedule and lifestyle alterations and to get used to the idea of an attention-thwarting, Mommy-monopolizing infant entering the picture. Here are a few things I recommend taking into consideration.

1. Create an open forum. Be forthcoming about the adjustments and changes your toddler is about to experience, because there's a lot for *her* to expect when you're expecting too!

Even though, for all intents and purposes, your toddler should remember exactly what it entails to be a baby (wasn't that just yesterday?), she won't. Your child needs to be told that brand-new babies should be held gently, can't crawl or walk or talk yet, need frequent diaper changes, and often screech like a barn owl in the middle of the night. A toddler is already a grown-up in her own mind, albeit one with really stunted growth. What *you* see is someone who still can't reach the bathroom sink, needs to hold your hand in parking lots, still requests bedtime stories and a night-light, and refuses to eat her vegetables. What *she* sees is someone who's wearing big-girl underpants, putting on her own pajamas, pumping her legs on the swing, and memorizing her alphabet. All of these achievements lead to the impression her infancy was a lifetime ago, so the idea of babyhood barely registers anymore. Some of the most memorable comments in our house have begun with someone under the age of four uttering the phrase "Mommy, remember when I was a little girl?"

With that in mind, keep the lines of communication open. Don't be afraid to let your toddler know what life was like when you were pregnant with him. Looking through photos from his babyhood is a great way to connect the dots too! Encourage frequent dialogue and questions, even if it means you have to come up with some sort of explanation for where babies come from.

2. Recognize breastfeeding can be a touchy subject. Sometimes quite literally. Even if your child is no longer dining at the breastaurant, it's tough to watch someone else enjoy a five-course meal.

Some children develop a bit of an ownership complex, which is totally normal. Though Gray had already weaned from breastfeeding by the time Marlowe was born, some mild envy surfaced when she saw her new sister partaking. She wasn't thrilled to have someone else sidling up to her favorite booby bar, so she started absentmindedly pawing at one of my breasts while her sister drank from the other side. Since that sort of overstimulation wasn't really on my agenda, I gently moved her hand away and suggested she lean her head against my shoulder and keep me company. It took a while for her to accept the change, but eventually she stopped trying to go to second base every time her sister was having a meal.

Before you add *Thou shalt not covet thy mother's breast* to the growing list of sibling commandments, try to remember part of the breastfeeding ritual—or bottle-feeding ritual, for that matter—between you and your older child involved offering comfort, security, and an opportunity to bond. It wasn't just about sustenance. While your older child may no longer require your breast milk for nourishment, he may feel bummed about no longer having your breasts to himself. (I'm sure your husband has felt that way once or twice since you started procreating too.)

Be honest with your toddler about what to expect in the breastfeeding department. I spent a lot of time reminding Gray that I would be feeding her sister from my breasts, just as I'd fed her. She asked a lot of questions, which I appreciated, because it meant she was absorbing and processing. I also kept a "breastfeeding box" on hand, filled with little treasures that were offered only while I was nursing the new baby. Having special toys and activities reserved for this purpose, such as puzzles and coloring books, provided a distraction Gray looked forward to. It also gave us a chance to interact even as I was nursing Marlowe.

3. Incorporate your toddler in every bit of preparation in which he's willing to participate. There's power in feeling involved. When Brad and I got married, we did our best to include all our family members in one capacity or another. We had several of our siblings sing or do readings during the wedding ceremony, for example. This was in an effort to give everyone a stake in our marriage. Sure, the marital union is technically between Brad and me, but our families continually reinforce it. Their love and support strengthen our commitment and help to keep it on course.

The same can be said for your firstborn child in regards to his sibling. Cultivating your first child's emotional investment, even before his sibling is born, will establish and intensify their connection. We had Gray help us with everything we could think of, from drawing a picture for her sister's nursery to attending prenatal visits (she was super excited to see the ultrasound and hear her sister's heartbeat!) and the baby shower. Even simple things, such as having your toddler help you organize the newborn clothes, hang a nursery mobile, or shop for crib sheets, will make him feel like a vital part of the process. Also—and this is a big one—be sure to encourage your toddler to rub your belly, talk to the baby, tell stories, and even sing. It's never too early to develop that sibling bond!

Another cool way to prepare your toddler is to practice feeding, washing, and diapering baby dolls. Gray's day care introduced us to this idea, and she took to it immediately. She also took it very seriously! It instilled a sense of responsibility within her and energized her nurturing side. Granted, she couldn't wait to dump buckets of water on her new sister's head upon arrival, courtesy of the doll-bathing practice at school, but I still considered it a victory.

4. Be proactive about major transitions. Sizable changes, such as moving your toddler from a crib to a bed, are often side effects of making way for a new family member. But they can also be the catalyst for insecurities. These adjustments may seem like a natural next step to you, but your toddler will view them like a sudden shifting of tectonic plates.

In the months leading up to Marlowe's birth, we transitioned Gray to her own room. Instead of apologizing for the massive upheaval, and making her feel displaced, we made an exciting adventure of it. I took Gray on an outing to choose her own paint colors and linens—which was *way* more fun for a two-year-old than one might've imagined! So what if we wound up with a purple-and-yellow theme reminiscent of a Laker jersey? Allowing her to participate in such a grown-up way made her feel honored. In fact, she was so proud of her choices, she couldn't wait to show everyone her new bedroom! When one of my friends complimented her new comforter, she even declared, "Thanks. It's from Target."

Start transitioning early, and do your best to recruit your toddler to assist you. In the long run it's helping you make way for Baby, while simultaneously promoting your toddler's maturity!

5. Don't blame the baby. It's really easy to tell your child changes are occurring because a new family member is on his way. However, it's important to make sure any associated adjustments are being viewed in a positive manner, without "blaming" your new arrival. This includes weaning from breastfeeding, altering sleeping arrangements, and any modification of the day care schedule.

As I mentioned earlier, we moved Gray into her own room before Marlowe was born. Instead of telling her she was being uprooted to make room for Marlowe, we explained she was becoming such a big girl that it was time to graduate to a "big-girl bed." We also helped her make the move well in advance of Marlowe's birth to create some psychological distance from it. This softened the blow and kept her from harboring any ill will toward her new sister over being ousted from her comfort zone.

There's no sense in pitting siblings against one another before they've even met! I promise, they'll find plenty of ways to accomplish that on their own in the near future.

6. Set aside surprises by having a few gifts on hand. Presents may seem like a shallow way to broach the subject of a new sibling, but your firstborn needs to feel special and included. Nothing says *I love you* like hugs, kisses, and a Whoopee Cushion!

I'm not saying you need to give your child a gift every time the baby receives one, but every now and then isn't a bad idea. It'll be tough for your toddler to see the baby getting fun things he's not allowed to touch or try out. He'll wonder why he's not supposed to play in the newly decorated nursery that's jam-packed with stuffed animals and unopened toys and looks like the most inviting place he's seen since you took him to that birthday party at Chuck E. Cheese. A small token might help ease the exclusion blues.

I do, however, recommend reserving gift giving for special moments of your choosing, rather than when the new baby gets a present. It's important for your older child to understand he won't always get something just because his brother or sister does; otherwise, it sets the stage for some serious expectations and competition!

Don't go to hospital hell in a hand basket.

When it comes time to introduce your toddler to his new baby brother or sister, there are a few factors to take into consideration so things go smoothly. Here are a few ideas that worked well for us.

1. Take a hospital tour. With any luck, your hospital offers a toddler tour. This was the single most helpful way we introduced Gray to the idea of having a sister!

Our tour began with a brief instructional class, with child-friendly explanations about a baby's development. It introduced Gray to proper terminology, allowed her to practice her doll-holding skills, and showed her there were other children her age having siblings too. She was so proud! The kids were taken on a tour of the maternity ward and shown where Mommy and the new baby would be staying for a few days. She also learned how she should hold her new baby sister, supporting her head and neck. Mind you, she was only two at the time, so we weren't planning on giving her any solo babysitting gigs. But it was beneficial information for her to file away nonetheless.

Because I can't resist sharing a cute story . . . During the toddler tour, the kids visited the nursery where the brand-new infants were being kept. A few were in their bassinets, and all the children pressed their faces against the glass to catch a glimpse of the intriguing, Onesie-sheathed creatures who were gurgling, burbling, drooling, and emitting tiny cries. The kids were in awe.

"This is where your new baby will be checked out by the nurses and doctors," the guide explained. A nurse then held one of the babies up, and the kids *oohed* and *aahed* like he was Simba in *The Lion King*.

When the guide moved on to the next attraction, worry lines appeared on my daughter's face. She began to whimper.

"What's wrong, Gray?" I asked.

"I thought we were taking the baby home today," she cried. "Where are they taking my baby?"

"Your baby sister is still in my tummy," I told her. "She's not quite ready to come out yet. That baby belongs to someone else."

"But I want *that* baby!" she wailed as all the other touring parents chuckled.

Fortunately, she soon forgot about the little guy. In a stealthy move that turned out to be the magic curator of sibling pride, the guide handed Gray a "Big Sister" T-shirt. She was so stoked, I'm not sure she took it off for the next three days! Kudos to you, good people at our local hospital . . . Do you make house calls?

2. Be understanding of elevated emotional levels. Toddler insecurities often manifest as anger. Hell, sometimes my insecurities do too!

According to the informational sheet we were given during Gray's toddler tour, it's normal and okay for children to be angry over the prospect of a new sibling. They need to know it's not an invalid feeling, and they shouldn't be punished for it. However, they *also* need to know it's *not* okay to hurt the baby under any circumstances.

During the aforementioned hospital tour, they gave us a "sibling adjustment" handout that listed possible behavioral changes a child might experience. Among them were stuttering, biting, pushing, whining and tantrums (isn't that the definition of being a toddler anyway?), asking for a bottle or wanting to breastfeed again, having nightmares, wetting the bed, and my favorite—suggesting "It" be sent back to the hospital. Obviously, we all hope to avoid any sort of neuroses or baby-related idiosyncrasies, but major changes sometimes result in uneasiness, a feeling of displacement, and/or minor displays of acting out.

When my husband was around four, my mother-in-law received a phone call from his preschool. Apparently, he'd begun spitting on some of his classmates. The school inquired if any major changes were occurring at home that might precipitate such an action, and my mother-in-law informed them she'd just had another baby. They suggested the spitting might be attributed to the adjustment of having to share his parents; to no longer being an only child. Fortunately, the spitting habit didn't last. The way I see it, it was replaced with other habits such as washing shirts with pens still in the pocket, collecting exorbitant numbers of flashlights, and leaving shoes in the middle of the bedroom floor, but who's counting?

Lashing out doesn't mean a child is bad, already hates his new sibling, or isn't a good brother or sister. It's a not-so-subtle cry for attention. So hang up on the child psychologist, and channel that patience!

3. Make interim babysitting arrangements that involve as little change as possible. You'll be staying in the hospital for a few days to have the new baby, so it stands to reason you'll be enlisting the help of a temporary guardian for your older child during that time. There's already an abundance of adjustments for your toddler to make, so it's great if you can stick to a routine that appeals to his level of comfort.

We did our best to keep Gray on her preexisting day care program when Marlowe was born, and we made sure she was being watched at home instead of elsewhere. This meant she was sleeping in her own bed, following the typical daily schedule, and surrounded by her canine BFFs. Any attempt you can make to adhere to normal structure will be hugely beneficial.

It's also important to ensure your toddler is being cared for by someone with whom he or she is comfortable. We were blessed to have my mom fill those shoes for us, as we knew Gray would feel unconditionally supported and loved even though we weren't at home with her.

4. Have the hospital staff put a photo of your older child in the new baby's crib. This idea was actually offered up by the hospital in which I gave birth, and I was grateful. Putting a photo of Gray in the bassinet with Marlowe was a sweet way for Big Sister to "watch over" Little Sister. It also allowed Gray to recognize which baby was "hers" when passing by the maternity ward nursery for the first time!

5. Introduce everyone ASAP, and visit often. My mom brought Gray to visit us every afternoon while we were in the hospital with Marlowe, per our request. We knew Gray was excited to see her sister, but part of it was selfish; we missed her terribly! It was hard to be away from one baby in order to welcome the other to the family. We also wanted Gray to immediately recognize the updated family dynamic and not feel threatened by it. Most importantly, we never wanted her to doubt how loved she is . . . new baby or not!

You'll likely feel exhausted and drained following the birth process, so your toddler's visit doesn't need to last longer than *War and Peace*. The point is to create an opportunity for everyone to bond, to promote family love on all fronts, and to encourage sibling acceptance to start working its way in.

6. Put the baby in a bassinet when your toddler arrives. Separation from Mommy and Daddy can make a child's emotions swing more than the Golden Gate Bridge. To keep jealousy at bay, and indulge your toddler's need for some meaningful mommy time, it's best to let your oldest say hello and give you overzealous hugs *before* having baby join the huddle.

7. Prepare a gift exchange. The idea isn't to bribe your toddler into accepting the new baby; it's to exchange an offering of love between new siblings. It doesn't have to be anything life-altering, and your infant will certainly never remember it, but having your kids give each other a small token of affection will be memorable for your toddler. Gray gifted Marlowe a cute little outfit, while Marlowe gave Gray a book celebrating sisterhood and a photo album to hold their first pictures together. Even now, you'd be surprised at how often they take time to sit and look through it together!

8. Let the show-and-tell begin. Becoming a big brother or sister is a very special honor, (hopefully your toddler will agree), and part of the fun is getting to spread the good news!

You know how you called/Facebook messaged/IMed/texted everyone just shy of your favorite Starbucks barista to let them know when the baby was born? Your toddler probably has an innate urge to do something similar. Gray was so over the moon when Marlowe was born, she started telling strangers on the street and begged to wear her Big Sister shirt to school all week. If I hadn't sent her in with celebratory goodies to dole out to her classmates, she might've resorted to carrier pigeons and smoke signals. Kids may not be able to pass out cigars but a small commemorative item or treat goes a long way! If you have a chance to prep handouts or a show-and-tell item (you know, in all that prelabor free time you have as you juggle chasing after your toddler, decorating a nursery, and waddling to the bathroom every five minutes), your toddler's pride will puff up like kettle corn.

9. Have a fun activity or destination waiting. Let's be honest: virtually *anyplace* is more fun to a toddler than the hospital, but your child may have a difficult time leaving you behind. After visiting with you and the new baby, he may feel he's missing something by going home again. No one likes to feel uninvited to the party, even if that party involves catheter removal, lime Jell-O, and a wailing infant.

We tried to make parting less traumatic by making sure my mom had after-visit arrangements in place each time Gray came to see us. One day they went out for ice cream, another they went home to paint. Any distraction your appointed guardian can come up with is probably a good one!

The homestretch.

Getting your new baby in the front door of your abode is an accomplishment in and of itself. You've not only managed to keep your eldest child alive longer than any houseplant you've ever owned, but somewhere in that process you managed to convince yourself you were handling parenthood with enough pluck and moxie that popping out a second kid sounded like a good plan!

Here are a few thoughts and ideas to assist you in piloting your new home life as mommy to multiple tiny humans.

1. Reserve special mommy moments. Every child needs his

own, solo, one-on-one time. Sure, siblings need to learn to share your attention, affection, and lap space, but they also need to know your focus isn't *always* divided and that you aren't playing favorites. Treasuring alone time with each child will strengthen their individual bonds with you and solidify that you love, listen to, and support them. Set aside ten minutes to read to your toddler before bed while your spouse holds the baby, or have your hubby help your toddler brush her teeth so you can quietly nurse your newborn. These occasions will remind everyone they're cherished and valued by both Mommy *and* Daddy. Even giving your toddler odd jobs around the house will help him feel appreciated! Besides, what's the point of having more kids if you can't put them to work?

2. Expect the family framework to shift, and don't try to stop it. At some vulnerable juncture, you may find yourself resisting the change in family dynamic because you're concerned about what it'll do to your toddler's psyche. Or your own, for that matter. You may worry it'll break your already existing mother-child bond or wonder if your first kid would thrive better as an only child. But I firmly believe having brothers and sisters is a gift. Siblings, no matter how similar or dissimilar, contribute toward one another's growth!

My mother-in-law once told me about an article she'd read regarding the drastic difference between some siblings. In it, one woman said something like, "But they were born into the same family. Why are my kids so different?"

The response was something akin to, "Well, technically they *weren't* born into the same family, because your oldest was born an only child. Your second child was born into a family with an older sibling, so the dynamics changed. Part of who they are is shaped by that modification."

I hope your fears subside as soon as you see that sibling synergy emerge! If your oldest is anything like Gray, she'll jump into the big sister role so enthusiastically you'll feel like she's trying to poach your job. In fact, one day Gray told me, "Look, Mommy, I'm wearing your shoes. Now there are *two* mommies in the house!" Of course, that's a little too close to the truth for comfort. Our house is already estrogen-filled enough as it is, without two moms running the show. My poor outnumbered husband.

3. Recognize the genetics kinetics. As I mentioned earlier, all children are different; I'm not telling you anything you don't already know. But knowing that fact and accepting it are two completely different beasts. You've gleaned certain knowledge and gotten used to certain aspects of infancy and toddlerhood by being in the trenches with your oldest child. Because that experience is so ingrained in you, you might inadvertently expect similar things of your second child. For example, you might expect him to achieve milestones on a particular timeline. You might also expect him to have the same reactions and emotional responses, or have similar levels of understanding, creative expression, learning styles, and/or opinions. Try to resist that inclination! Throw everything you already know out the window. Actually, scratch that. File it all away in your happy place and/or your eldest child's baby book, and then offer your newborn a clean slate. It's very intimidating to live in your older sibling's shadow. Just ask Ron Howard's little brother! If you can remember his name.

4. Accept that juggling ain't just for circus folk. In a nutshell, here's what it's like to have two toddlers.

Me: "Gray, please put my heels back in my closet. You're going to break your ankle."

Gray: "But, Mom, I'm . . ."

Me: "Oh no! Marlowe, are you licking chalk? Really? Chalk?

Gray, that's why I shut the door to the front room. Why did you open it again?"

(I wipe off Marlowe's green-tinged tongue and remove the piece of chalk from her fist. She throws herself on the floor and begins crying hysterically as Gray rolls her eyes and considers an appropriate comeback.)

Gray: "Actually, it's not a door, Mom. It's a gate. So, you know, you're really wrong about that."

I beeline for a glass of wine before my head implodes. And . . . scene.

5. Expect kids to have an impeccable sense of timing. And by *impeccable*, I mean super crappy. The crappiest. Crappier than newspaper on the bottom of a gerbil cage. Toddlers are exceptionally gifted at coming up with new and improved ways to interrupt when you least want them to. Your child's uncanny sixth sense for disruption means he'll wait until his new baby sister is peacefully passed out in your arms (which was preceded by three straight hours of no-holds-barred, sleep-deprived, colic-induced caterwauling) before asking for a glass of milk, the only toy out of his reach, or the bathroom door to be opened. Any and all requests will be made loudly, with inflexible urgency, and in close proximity to the baby's eardrums. No amount of forethought will save you from this scenario—it's inevitable. But at least you'll know there are countless other mommies out there who sympathize! You know, if *sympathize* really means *wish all toddlers came equipped with a mute button.*

6. Foster the love. The fact is, I don't know what I would do without my own siblings. Truly. They are three of the kindest, wittiest, most talented people on this planet. They possess more cool in their pinkie toes than I possess in my entire body, and I mean that with zero read-between-the-lines sarcasm or my typical snark.

Do we fight sometimes? Abso-freaking-lutely. But we also have an unparalleled, untouchable, inextricable bond.

I can certainly vouch for Gray and Marlowe's close-knit connection, and if you're blessed with more than one child, I hope your children will be able to say the same. Even if listening to them fight is only slightly more fun than bathing in kitty litter.

One of my most cherished photos. The pride Gray had over holding her new baby sister for the first time was both profound and precious.
Photo courtesy of Jenna von Oy.

Bond. Sibling Bond.

Basically, siblings are double the trouble and double the love. Just when you think your kids are going to beat each other senseless over who uses the purple comb or who gets the last strawberry, they become bona fide allies that gang up on you like the Mafia.

I recently read an article that stated the following: "Did you know that research has shown that healthy sibling relationships can significantly benefit us later in life? Those with positive sibling relationships report higher life satisfaction and lower rates of depression later in life. Also in times of illness and traumatic events, siblings provide emotional, social, and psychological support to each other. Research shows that this support is common regardless of whether they live next to or far away from each other."[8]

When I had my girls, I didn't expect the sibling bond to surface so early on. I envisioned an entertaining future of spirited sparring matches over hair dryers, makeup, boyfriends, and who gets the bathroom first, but I never anticipated such a closeness from day one. I was astounded. Even before they could communicate with words, my girls had an unspoken dialogue even my husband and I felt left out of.

It's not that we expected Gray to shun Marlowe, but my husband and I approached our new family dynamic with open minds and a lot of love. Just in case. Even caring, happy-go-lucky siblings can experience some jealousy!

Gray quickly made us realize we'd worried needlessly. She devoted herself to sisterhood in ways I'd never dreamed. In fact, when Marlowe was just shy of two months old, Gray asked me, "Mommy, did Santa bring me my little sister for Christmas?" (Naturally, I answered yes, because I'm such a people pleaser.)

8 "Healthy Sibling Relationships," Psychology Today, April 26, 2014, accessed August 1, 2016, https://www.psychologytoday.com/blog/teen-angst/201404/healthy-sibling-relationships.

Her inquiry was slightly misguided, but isn't it cool she thought of her new little sister as a gift?

Another time she informed me, "Mommy, Marlowe wants *me* to put on her socks and shoes today. She thinks I'm a tiny grown-up." (She's not the only one, kid!)

I realize not all children will be easygoing or feel like Gray did at the beginning, and that's perfectly normal. Sometimes kids don't start bonding until they can interact with one another more easily. In other words, your baby may need to crawl, walk, or talk a bit before big brother wants anything to do with her. Give it some time. Before you know it, she'll be the yin to his yang.

Before Marlowe was old enough to do much other than sleep, cry, and poop (rewind, repeat), Gray nominated herself to act as my sidekick, Mini-Mom, part-time dog herder, clean diaper retriever, cuddler, car seat pacifist, bath-time soother, lullaby crooner, and spontaneous hug giver (because "I just love her soooo much, Mommy, I can't help it—I *have* to squeeze her!").

She wasn't the only one who was moved by the love. The feeling was, incontrovertibly, mutual. If I wanted Marlowe to smile for a photo, all I had to do was prop her up in front of Gray, and voilà! She'd smile like the Cheshire cat. Even as an infant, Mar would reach over to grab her sister's hand or immediately look around for her when she awoke from a nap. In a way, they've always belonged to one another. Even better, their friendship has only grown. Now it's Sisterhood 2.0, and it's profoundly beautiful. Well, until it's not. But that's a story for a different section.

Wonder twin powers activate.

Having two kids means they teach one another everything; it's eternal follow the leader. Sometimes this is equivalent to Tom Brady leading the New England Patriots to victory; other times it's Custer's

Last Stand. And we aren't just talking about the influence of an older child over a younger one here. Sometimes younger siblings can be more dominant than Julius Caesar.

For example, Marlowe's fearlessness often convinces Gray to try things she's otherwise unnerved by. The moment she witnesses her little sister jumping on a trampoline, or careening down a giant corkscrew slide like an Olympic bobsledder, Gray throws caution to the wind and queues up right behind her.

When my little sister, Alyssa, and I were younger, we took a summer gymnastics camp together. She was always far more athletically inclined than I was (still is), so it motivated me. Oh, who am I kidding? It stirred my bullheaded, übercompetitive impulses like a tennis match between Serena and Venus. On day one of our camp, Alyssa did an effortless, pristine, no-handed cartwheel on her first try. This pissed me off royally, given I'd already attempted it several times without success . . . well, unless *success* is skinning one's knee, banging one's elbow on a balance beam, and face planting so hard one gets rug burn all the way up to her eyeballs. But when I heard the round of applause my sister received for her impressive trick, I turned right around and did a no-handed cartwheel too. You gotta love the thrill of one-upmanship! And hubris.

My girls are constantly engaged in healthy antagonism and teaming up in the pursuit of fun . . . also known as *getting in trouble*. One day I overheard Gray, who was three at the time, tell her one-year-old sister, "Marlowe, don't do the stuff I do, okay? Because we're not really supposed to do it."

Thanks to Gray, Marlowe has taken a huge interest in constructive activities such as reading books, dancing unabashedly, getting herself dressed, attempting potty training, and brushing her teeth. Of course, she has also learned how to jump on the bed, climb on furniture and dogs, raid my closet for "dress-up" clothes, and swing from the *Oh, shit!* handle in my car. Which I've dubbed the *Uh-oh!* handle instead, for obvious reasons.

Brothers and sisters encourage each other in both positive and negative ways, and you can't really have one without the other. So get ready. Breaking up brawls and staving off bickering is your new occupational hazard!

It takes two to tango. And torture.

My mom used to tell people she had an even number of kids so everyone would have someone to play and fight with. I mentioned that to a fellow mom recently, and she responded with, "Oh, I have three kids, and they've never been at a loss for someone to fight with."

This may sound daft, but innocent sibling quibbling is actually a good thing! Provided, of course, the clashes in question don't result in a leg cast or 911 call. In my opinion, harmless disputes strengthen the sibling bond. They teach children how to interact, set boundaries, share, and respect the opinions of others. They also help each child learn that love ultimately transcends any issue that might arise.

Expecting children to bypass arguments altogether is about as practical as underwear on a donkey. But that doesn't mean we should tolerate toxic practices. We mommies have to promote fair and gentle sibling behavior! Here are a few sibling issues we're dealing with (so far) at our house that I'm trying to curb. Please note I said *trying.* I'm a mom, not a magician.

1. Tattling. My girls spill the beans on one another about everything from who ran down the hallway, to who smeared banana on the couch, to who broke my favorite necklace while using it as a jump rope. Half the time, they overdramatize their snitching more than a Mexican soap opera.

Typically, Gray is my resident gossipmonger, blurting things such as "Mommy, Marlowe's trying to wash her hands in toilet water again!" But Marlowe has her moments too. Even when she only possessed ten words in her vocabulary, she would scream "Mama!" and point disdainfully at her sister. Now *that's* some sign language I don't need an interpreter for.

My favorite tattling story comes from one of my best friends, who has two sons. She and I went out for a cocktail one evening (better known as a much-needed break involving grown-up conversation) while our husbands watched the kids (better known as ignoring the tiny humans who were ransacking the house, while immersing themselves in *Huffington Post* headlines). My friend and I got into a conversation about how siblings amp each other up.

"We were staying at an Airbnb once, and the owner was there overseeing a plumbing issue," my friend began. "Suddenly, my oldest came running into the room blabbing, 'Mom, Chuck just said *fuck*, and now he's peeing all over the living room floor.'"

"I was sure Chuck hadn't dropped the F-bomb," she continued. "My oldest just wanted an excuse to swear in front of me without getting punished. The peeing was a totally different story—that was *definitely* going down. He was in there christening the Airbnb, right in front of the homeowner. I swear, nothing makes my boys turn it on more than when guests come over. They like to put on a show."

I thought back to every time my girls have acted like aliens in front of company and took another sip (gulp) of my drink.

"Take it from me," she finished, "the minute those guests walk out, you'll get your kids back. They go from punks to monks in a matter of seconds."

So basically, if you think the tattling is bad when no one else is around, expect the worst when you have complete strangers over!

2. Instigation and provocation. Attention seeking comes in a plethora of exciting forms. Whether it's hitting, pushing, yelling, hiding each other's socks, or throwing one another's toys across the room, my daughters push each other's buttons big time. Almost as much as they push mine.

The following phrase actually came out of my mouth: "Hey! We don't pluck our sister's eyelashes, pinch her skin, bite her nose, stick things in her belly button, or floss her teeth with our toes. Hugs and kisses *only*, please." We have a lot of fun at our house.

As it turns out, mastering the art of harassing one's sibling does *not* have age restrictions. Even as an infant, Marlowe knew how to goad her big sister. When I breastfed her on the couch each morning, she would close her eyes and pretend to be asleep. When everyone else appeared distracted, she would subtly inch her feet toward Gray's rib cage, then abruptly dig her toes in. As soon as Gray cried out in pain and annoyance, I would look down to see Marlowe slyly grinning as she drank. Evidently, she enjoyed a bit of badgering with her breakfast.

The range of instigation has only grown (though not matured) along with my girls. The older they get, the more passionate their rabble-rousing appears to be. When she was eighteen months, with no provocation, Marlowe ripped out a massive wad of Gray's hair. It was such an enormous clump I almost stuffed it in her baby book and labeled it *Gray's First Hair Cut*. Similarly, our New Year's photos from 2015 consist almost entirely of Marlowe yanking out Gray's barrettes and poking her sister in the eye. I can't wait for them to start trading clothes and curling irons.

3. Forgetting to share. Though please feel free to substitute the word *forgetting* with the more apropos technical term *refusing*.

Sharing is one of those things that can often pit siblings against one another. Sharing the blame? Always. Sharing toys? Sometimes.

Sharing the last cookie from the jar? Never. If you even suggest it, you must have a screw loose.

In our family, when opportunities to share make our girls scrappy, we first suggest taking turns. When that doesn't work, and a technical knockout is imminent, we separate them and force-feed some alone time to everyone involved. It usually doesn't take long before they're hugging it out and finding some other unique form of torture to inflict upon one another. Or me.

4. *Jealousy and fairness.* Kids have a warped sense of what's *fair*. In my daughters' eyes, fair is something villainous. *Fair* is what it's called when your little sister wants a turn with the Slinky and you feel like hoarding it in your pocket even though you aren't playing with it anymore and Mommy makes you hand it over to be *fair*. This scenario unfailingly leads to the ever-popular (and whiny) toddler tagline "But that's not fair!" and is often followed by a meltdown so astronomical it'll give you the shakes.

In my house, *It's not fair* is a refrain that's endlessly and gratingly chanted when things aren't going my kids' way. It's often tossed out as a last resort, and it usually means things are in a galaxy far, far away from *actually* being unfair. Things are the antithesis of unfair, even. Because a toddler's definition of *fair* is *Who gives a flip if there's collateral damage, as long as I get what I want?*

My girls have been known to complain about the *unfairness* of not being allowed to play outside in the middle of a January blizzard, to overflow the bathtub with soapsuds, or to paint landscapes on our refrigerator with eyeliner they stole from my makeup bag. And my favorite car ride gripe? "Mommy, it isn't fair that we're listening to music *you* want to hear. I want to listen to 'Happy' again!" (Don't get me wrong. I adore Pharrell; I think he's a genius. But when you hear the same song on repeat for hours on end, without intermission, it doesn't matter how much you dig the tune. Ain't nothing "Happy" about it.)

Apparently, we mommies should be forbidden from doing ridiculous things like listening to music we enjoy, taking a quiet bubble bath, getting through an entire chapter of a book in one sitting, or swallowing a bite of dinner before being begged to fetch additional items from the kitchen. In my humble opinion, mommies should be able to do all of those things and more. But what do I know? According to my kids I'm *unfair*.

5. *Name-calling.* I'm not going to lie, most of the time the so-called "naughty" names my kids invent in the heat of the moment are so damn funny I have to pinch myself to keep from snorting coffee out my nose. My reigning favorites are *Poo-poo Head, Princess Pottyface,* and the dreaded *Stupid Hippopotamus Booger Butt*! Also, do you notice a theme? Nearly all toddler trash-talking involves toilet-related humor.

It's true: the goofy names my kids have come up with for one another could be worse. In fact, they don't come close to a few creative ones I've muttered under my breath while crossing paths with some of the jackassery out there. Nonetheless, I try to teach my children to speak kindly to one another. Silly terms of endearment are one thing, but if I sense my girls are using names to be insulting, I try to steer them in a slightly less profane direction. You know what works best for me? Ad-libbing the most absurd combination of innocuous words I can think of. I'm particularly fond of *Stinkerpatootie* and *Li'l Miss Persnickety Picklepants*. These aren't entirely out of the name-calling woods, I suppose, but they're certainly less offensive than some. They also tend to make my kids giggle so hard they forget all about being angry. Score!

THE MORAL OF MY STORY

Introducing a new baby to the family can be equal parts elation and trepidation. Your children might wind up being partners in crime, troublemakers in arms, argument allies, or accomplices of the rambunctious kind. Or perhaps even a combination thereof. But with any luck, they'll also be the best of friends!

Don't be dismayed if it takes some time to work up to that camaraderie. The old cliché rings true: *Good things come to those who wait.* Good sibling-bond-promoting but parent-alienating things. Like covering for one another when they try beer for the first time, sneaking out after midnight, and plotting ragers while you're out of town. But who knows? If luck is on your side, maybe they'll also pool together to pay for a really nice assisted living facility for you when you're eighty-five. And what mom wouldn't appreciate that?

Gray crashes my interview with *E!* and my inner multitasker goes into serious overdrive. *Photo courtesy of Jenna von Oy.*

CHAPTER 11
Working and Harried . . . with Children

A SCENIC VIEW OF MY PAST

People often ask what I found to be the most grueling part of being a "child star." Obviously, my standard response is, "Going to red carpet events, reading ego-boosting fan mail, meeting famous people, getting free shit, and working with Joey Lawrence—looking at his face every day was simply intolerable!"

Oh, simmer down, Joey Lawrence fans; I kid. I had a ginormous crush on the guy too. In fact, I plastered posters of him on my bedroom walls just like the rest of you gals did. (And some of the gents out there as well, I imagine.) Unlike the rest of you, I had to remember to shove those posters under my bed whenever he came over for a visit. Not that I'm saying he visited often—the adolescent me should have been so lucky. Either way, it might've been a little awkward if he'd caught me practicing my French kissing "skills" all over his face when he *did* come over. Man, thirteen was a weird age.

Anyway, the most burdensome part of being a young actor certainly wasn't whatever "sacrifices" I made—those were by choice. Missing homecoming games, proms, birthdays . . . that sort of thing was never a big deal to me; we all make concessions for our jobs. And, to be totally fair, how burdened can one really be when one is being paid to be on a freaking top-ten television show? I was doing okay for myself.

The thing that weighed heavily was being away from my family for extended periods of time. As I mentioned in the last chapter, part of my family remained in Connecticut, while the other half of us lived in Los Angeles during my work season. And that opened the door for a lot of homesick heartache.

During one particular hiatus week in 1991, my mom and Tyler and I traveled back to rural Connecticut to spend some much-needed time with the rest of the family. I was relieved to be out of the limelight for a bit—back in Newtown, where I'd grown up. It's a small town that has always offered just the right amount of enthusiasm regarding my success—everyone supported me but didn't waste time propping me up on some sort of flashy pedestal I didn't belong on. Going home was always the precise dose of humility I needed. Just when I got too caught up in the Hollywood bullshit (thought my character had too few lines in a *Blossom* episode, was bummed the show didn't win an Emmy, or felt jilted because I'd lost yet another movie role to Jennifer Love Hewitt), I went back to Newtown to get centered.

My hometown couldn't have hit me harder with perspective if it had wielded a Louisville Slugger. I could immerse myself in petty middle school gossip, peruse the mystery novel aisle at our local library, catch a two-dollar movie at the town hall, pick raspberries and blackberries from our backyard patch, ride bikes with my siblings until sundown, and hear my dad sing in the church choir. Most importantly and cathartically, I could spend hours on end hugging on, and laughing with, my family. I felt like I had permission to do normal things for a while. Sometimes a trivial exchange like "Hey, Alyssa, can you please pass the butter?" was so therapeutic, I was moved to the point of tears. At home, I was "Just Jenna." I wasn't the girl in teenybopper magazines who fielded shouts of *Whoa!* and wore the hell out of ridiculous hats.

Which is why it was even more confusing and hurtful when someone burst that bubble.

One afternoon, while my dad was at the grocery store and my mom was doing laundry, the phone rang. I lifted it off the receiver. "Hello, who's calling, please?" (Only in my wildest dreams can I convince my own kids to answer the phone that politely . . .)

The guy on the other end of the line introduced himself as my brother's karate teacher. "Who is this?" he asked.

"I'm Peter's sister, Jenna," I told him with swelling, big sisterly pride.

"Oh, you're that actress girl," he said with no trace of cordiality. I'd never met the guy, but he didn't sound like he was a *Blossom* fan. Or a fan of mine in general, for reasons unknown to me.

I tried to adhere to polite tactics. "Would you like to speak to my mom or my brother?" I asked.

"Yes," he answered, "but before I do, you should know it's terrible that you never show up to support your brother at his karate lessons. Family is more important than some stupid Hollywood show, and you're not a good sister. He's going to resent you for that someday."

His words were a launched grenade, and they rocked me to the core. Heat rose to my face, my lip started trembling, and I did my best to keep from bursting into tears. I'd never been spoken to that way before. Moreover, I was devastated at the suggestion I was an uninvolved sister, that I didn't love my brother enough. I spent a lot of time acting like a mature adult, given my career, but I was still only fourteen years old. Good grief, I still wore training bras and kept zit cream on my nightstand! What did this guy expect from me? I wasn't even old enough to drive myself to Pete's lessons.

Up until that moment, I thought I'd been pretty successful at being an encouraging, loving big sister. I was under the impression I'd been appropriately and genuinely supportive of my siblings' endeavors, despite a full-time workload, school schedule, and living nearly three thousand miles away. I love them with all my heart, and I'd done everything in my power to attend everything I could. But the impact of a stranger's judgment can be psychologically annihilating, no matter how misdirected. As if Hollywood hadn't already done enough to shake my self-confidence, that dude doused it with kerosene and set it ablaze.

I was so filled with shame that day, I never even told my parents about the conversation. You know why? Because my own guilt surfaced from the depths like a nuclear submarine, and my own guilt was *far* more destructive than anything Mr. Asshat Karate Instructor could ever say to me.

CUT TO . . .

Missing out on family time to be a working kid was tough. Missing out on family time to be a working mom is the epitome of heartbreaking.

Mommy guilt is a powerful thing. Despite a profoundly deep love for my career, those sad little faces gut me like a mackerel every time I leave for a day of writing or filming. You can prepare yourself for a tedious PowerPoint presentation, the wrath of El Niño during your only time off, and a hostile takeover by a band of hipsters at your favorite local coffee shop that has free Wi-Fi. But there's simply no way to prepare oneself for the sheer, unrelenting, overwhelming force of toddler love. It's mightier than the gravitational pull of Jupiter.

MY CRADLE CHRONICLES

Like many of you, or perhaps most of you, I'm a working mom. Technically speaking, I'm a full-time working, stay-at-home mom, so I suppose that makes me a "work-from-home mom." What does that mean, exactly? If you go to an office each day, it probably means your desk doesn't have stale rice puffs and baby drool all over it like mine does. Or a monitor doubling as a paperweight. Or "autographs" on your contract pages in crayon. But I imagine our stories are similar nonetheless. Having my desk at home only gets me a few steps closer to my coffee pot and a pantry full of snacks. And a private toilet. And maybe sneaking in an episode of *Castle* during my lunch break, without my boss or coworkers breathing down my neck.

Now, before you go thinking I've got it made (crazy talk!), did you forget I mentioned I'm trying to get work done while simultaneously taking care of two wily toddlers? The only reason no one is breathing down my neck is because they're too busy scampering through the house like woodland creatures on speed, tearing shit apart, and fighting over who looks better in the toilet paper tutu. And for the record, they micromanage my time more than any executive I've ever known. They veto my ideas, hijack my phone conversations, and never allow me enough time for lunch (is there a union for that?). Oh, and that *private* toilet I referenced? It's not quite so private when you have to pry kids off your leg like a tongue stuck to a frozen light pole.

Whether you're a working mom, a stay-at-home-mom, or a combination thereof, I have no doubt you're working your butt off.

Getting All Worked Up

Here are a few terms I find go hand-in-hand with being a working mom. That is, if *working* is loosely defined as trying to get *anything* done while kid wrangling.

In other words, you should be able to relate to this whether you're the CEO of a Fortune 500 company or of your own household. Or both.

1. Prioritizing. In general, being a parent means you learn to prioritize the crap out of your life. This often translates to a whole lot of saying no. You'll say no to back-to-back birthday parties (too much cake, too little time for napping), no to dinner with your girlfriends when the kids are puking (even though that's when you need a night out even more than you need to chug preemptive Theraflu), and no when someone suggests a family vacation to a cabin in the mountains. (Because the only thing worse than cabin fever in your *own* home is cabin fever in someone else's. Especially since they may not place as much value as you do on maintaining a fully stocked bar.)

No becomes a crucial word in your vocabulary so you can maintain a feasible schedule and your mental marbles. If your answer to a request or invitation isn't in the *Hell, yes!* category, then it might start to find itself in the *Hell, no!* category instead.

A toddler can easily turn into a good (and honest) excuse not to accept every proposal that comes along. Just because something sounds like fun doesn't mean it's the best way to spend your time at this stage of the game. And that's okay! How you prioritize your family and career is specific to you—only you know the most comfortable way to divide and conquer!

2. Good-bye, guilt. Nothing lights the guilt match quite like watching your toddler try to put on a brave face as she kisses you good-bye. It doesn't matter if you're dropping her off at day care so you can go to the office or leaving her with your parents so you can attend a weeklong conference. There's something about that quivering lip that'll play your heartstrings like a cello. Meet your new best friends, Sappy and Sentimental.

Guilt will creep in whether or not you have a desk job and whether your departure is born out of need or want. Hell, sometimes I feel bad leaving the girls with their dad so I can make a quick run to the pharmacy. And it's their *dad*, for Pete's sake! He's perfectly capable of taking care of our daughters, as long as he's not expected to pick out their clothes for school. Well, ones that match or make any sort of seasonal sense, that is.

It's tough to let ourselves off the hook for leaving our children in someone else's care, whether it's work-related or not. Our motherly instincts tell us we're the best person to watch over and protect our offspring. And rightfully so! It stands to reason we might have some apprehension about delegating that task to someone else. If you grieve each time you say good-bye, you aren't an anomaly or a weirdo. Well, I suppose you might be a weirdo; I don't really know. Either way, you aren't alone!

If, at any point, you've wondered whether I'm sitting back with a glass of vino, dictating every page of this book to a ghostwriter, let me give you a little insight. I wrote the bulk of this chapter while on a three-day/two-night trip to California for work. It was the first time I'd traveled without one or both of my girls—the first time I'd ever left my youngest at home. And while I must confess to giddily enjoying a glass of wine or two during my travels, and stretching out like Gumby in my hotel bed (I also slept so hard I drooled. Do you blame me?), I felt lost without my kids.

During the throes of bedlam back at home, I'd conjured up plenty of ideas about what I would do with "free time," should the universe ever take pity on me and grant me some. But lo and behold, when I finally had that freedom, I didn't know what the heck to do with it. I floundered. I mean, a mother can only sip so many cups of coffee or scroll through her Twitter feed for so long before she's a jittery mess with TMI on the goings-on of everyone else's pets and politics. Or before she thinks she hears phantom shouts of "Mommy, I have to go potty!" coming from the adjacent restaurant booth.

I tried really hard to appreciate the meditative quality of

traveling alone. I really did. And I was feeling pretty dang proud of my accomplishments. I even finished an entire book that didn't contain rhyming stanzas or start with "Once upon a time." Holy shit! But then, in an unfortunate turn of events, I managed to miss my layover in Houston on the trip back.

I was informed I would be waiting an additional twenty-four hours to hug my children. And that's when every passenger and flight attendant who passed through the George Bush Intercontinental Airport saw me openly weeping into my dinky, airline-donated travel toothbrush kit. "I just want to get home to my babies," I bawled in the middle of terminal C as I collected pockets full of Kleenex from sympathetic (and slightly unnerved) passersby.

It wasn't my best attempt at subtlety. From what I've been told, my kids handled my absence better than I did.

Accept that guilt is part of the deal, and try not to mercilessly nag yourself about it. As I mentioned in my first book, "Guilt is a bright-red, fire-breathing, foulmouthed beast that can crush your spirit. *If* you let it."

3. Flexibility. (Not the fun kind that makes for a mean game of drunken Twister or encourages your husband to buy you racy lingerie.) Giving ample time to all our home and work responsibilities can be a high-wire act! As I've mentioned in previous chapters, I'm not the biggest fan of change. That said, parenting is all about flexibility and adaptation. Becoming a mother has honed my "go with the flow" skills. Except, apparently, when I miss layovers in the Houston airport.

4. Dedication. Parenting and career paths both necessitate devotion and single-mindedness—the type reserved for passing the bar exam or becoming president of the United States. The caveat? Both work and family deserve 100 percent of your energy, so how does *that* math work? The answer is sometimes it doesn't. We make the best decisions we can in that moment, given the circumstances.

I believe you're on the right track as long as you approach both work and your parenting with dedication. You might be surprised at how often life allows them to assist one another! Sometimes the dedication we have for our children even comes out *through* our work. As an example, I wrote a good portion of the first *Situation Momedy* from my hospital bed after giving birth to Gray. Some women take maternity leave for three months. I took mine for less than three hours. I told you I love my work! Of course, you're welcome to blame that job dedication on the C-section meds they had me on; you probably aren't far off. But I'd also like to think jumping back into my work really served as a form of catharsis. I needed something to keep me busy while my sweet baby was stuck in the transitional nursery, and writing provided the perfect outlet. If I couldn't spend that time visiting my newborn and giving her round-the-clock kisses, at least I could get paid to write about her!

For some, dedication is pumping breast milk at work. For others, it's working a second job so one's child can take soccer or gymnastics. You might be putting in overtime while your baby naps so your boss will let you work remotely or taking the night shift so you can be with your kids during the day. You might find you're exhausted from working back-to-back shifts, but you take time to sing your kids to sleep anyway.

Dedication means something different for each of us, so give yourself credit where credit is due. Have faith in your efforts!

5. Passion. You don't owe anyone an apology for what you do, whether you choose to work full-time or part-time, or no time. It's okay to be passionate about your job—in fact, it's fantastic! Who says you can't love work *and* your kids simultaneously? In fact, I hope you treasure, appreciate, and feel inspired by *both*!

Most of the moms I know who continue following their dreams after having babies worry most about being selfish. Having a job doesn't mean you're being selfish; it means you're being self*less*! As my friend Jenn recently told me, "There's a reason flight attendants tell parents to put on their own oxygen mask before their children's."

It's easier to respect the position we hold in our marriages and parenting when we first respect ourselves and what drives us. For many of us, that self-respect is directly tied to our careers!

My dear friend, Cindy Alexander, who's an incredible singer/songwriter/mommy whom I admire greatly, once wrote a blog on the subject of leaving her children to go on tour. She wrote, "I am a better Mom and Wife because I don't deny my passion. . . . My energy and fuel comes from the creative firestorm that I allow myself to walk in and out of on a regular basis. It took a long time to get to this place of completely honoring myself as an Artist, and rather than living in a very delicate balance, it's more like climbing to the high part of the tipped scale to breathe and stretch a little in order to maintain my sanity. . . . I hope that my children will find the gift that comes not from another person, but from within — a 'super power' of sorts that assures them they can get through ANYTHING. Could be a sense of humor, could be the commitment to love relentlessly. Some people may call it Faith . . ."[9]

If nothing else, passion is having faith and pride in your own convictions—in the things that inspire, invigorate, and move you. I firmly believe passion in one area begets passion in others, including more passionate parenting. I feel I'm a better parent because I pursue my dreams. But passion doesn't necessarily have to come in the form of a paid job; that's an important distinction. It can come in the

9 Cindy Alexander, "My 'Super Power,'" Ponderings, March 29, 2016, accessed August 1, 2016.

form of journal writing, sewing, scrapbooking, painting, rescuing animals, nonprofit volunteering, or working out at the gym. No matter what shape it takes for you, do what you love and love what you do . . . including being a mom!

Working Moms and Stay-at-Home Moms: The Family Feud

Comparing and contrasting working moms versus stay-at-home moms seems to be a popular topic these days in the media-magnified mommy wars. I truly wish we could remove the term *mommy wars* from our pop culture lexicon altogether, but my magic wand doesn't appear to be working at the moment. The fact is, pitting working moms against stay-at-home moms isn't helping our already pressured and intense job of parenting. It's forcing us to choose sides, and it's leaving us with unfair and intolerant expectations of one another and ourselves.

The general implication seems to be that working moms ignore their children and/or choose their careers over actively participating in their children's lives. Alternately, the suggestion seems to be that stay-at-home moms have it easy because they choose not to work and/or don't appreciate the time they have with their kids when so many others aren't blessed with that luxury.

Those are unfortunate stigmas. We *all* work hard, ladies! Working doesn't make you a bad mom, and not working doesn't make you a less relevant parent. It also shouldn't suggest that neither party is allowed to acknowledge challenges or air grievances. No one should be ostracized for that!

I have no doubt you're pulling your weight. If you're being the best mom *you* know how to be, isn't that the important thing? The fact remains, what works for one family dynamic may not work for another. I know stay-at-home dads who kick serious ass, and working moms who spend as much quality time with their children as most stay-at-home moms do. It's all about what you do with the time you *do* have. And judging other moms certainly isn't the most productive way we can spend that time!

The Professional Standards Committee

You can be "professional" at a lot of things, and not all of them involve wearing a suit, having an assistant, or owning a briefcase. In other words, being a stay-at-home mom doesn't mean someone isn't a professional! Stay-at-home moms are professional glue-that-keeps-shit-together women—many households wouldn't function without them! If my mom hadn't been a stay-at-home mom, for example, I would never have wound up on a television series. Why? Because no one would've had the time to indulge my ambition. It takes all kinds of moms to make the world go round, and thank God for mine! (Except when she's behind the wheel of a motor vehicle or attempting to give me directions *anywhere*. But I suppose we all have our shortcomings.)

I know a lot of women—and men, for that matter—who erroneously believe stay-at-home moms have it easy. Oh, contraire, mon amie. If you're a stay-at-home mom, *every* day is Bring Your Kid to Work Day. And I ask you, what's so effortless about *that*? You think all-day pencil-pushing is backbreaking work? Try spending all day working to keep your toddler from pushing those pencils into every orifice on his body. Or equally bad—every orifice on *your* body. There's a lot more work involved in full-time parenting than most stay-at-home parents ever get credit for. I'm sure my mom would agree.

Just because someone is classified as a stay-at-home mom doesn't mean they're whiling away the hours reading Fabio-adorned romance novels as their kids "redecorate" every room of the house. Most of the time, those moms are displaying enough patience to rival the pope's and reflexes that would make Jean-Claude Van Damme do a double take. Sometimes those same moms are also diapering while daydreaming of a career they're wild about that's currently on the back burner. Not to mention, not all stay-at-home moms are "lucky" they don't have to work. Some have no choice because they can't afford day care.

Regardless of the reason behind one's need or desire to remain home with her children, stay-at-home moms have my utmost respect and admiration.

Work-from-home moms do their homework.

Home is a freelancer's Zen Den. I know this from personal experience, and I have a fondness for being able to get paid while existing in my comfort zone. It has been a blessing for my family and me. That said, I think the most common misconception about those of us who maintain a home office is that we can do *whatever* the hell we want, *whenever* the hell we want—including, but not limited to, filing paperwork in our pajamas, lunching with friends in lieu of answering e-mails, and doing a P90X workout while telecommuting. (I'm nowhere *near* that ambitious, but whatever rocks your socks, you overachiever, you!)

To a certain extent, all of those things might be true. A work-from-home mom's schedule often has a certain flexibility not frequently offered in, or associated with, an office setting. But it's important to keep in mind work-from-home moms are still . . . you guessed it, working! Despite some side benefits that only exist in the convenience and privacy of one's own home (such as going commando or openly belching), the work still has to be done. And, in some ways, self-imposed deadlines are more arduous to live up to than those set by others. Trust me on this, being at home can offer more distractions than a fluffle of Playboy Bunnies parading through a correctional facility.

Work-from-home moms tend to be taken less seriously, because we have easy access to our bed and our wine rack. But neither of those is getting much love (or any) on a workday, believe me! If I crawled into bed every time it looked enticing, this book would consist of only a dedication page and a chapter list.

I'm certainly not complaining, but even working in the sanctity of one's own home has pitfalls. Sometimes hibernating in comfort and convenience hinders progress. For instance, if I skip showering and/or don't get out of my nightgown, I don't get work done. My sanitation habits and dress code directly affect my mind-set. Studies have shown (don't ask me which ones; I learned this from my very well-read husband) there are psychological benefits to getting dressed when you work from home. Dressing for success heightens your self-worth. Which means, theoretically, you get more accomplished! It makes sense when you think about it. Our subconscious is hung up on being a creature of comfort, and that creature would happily trade a cubicle and some water cooler gossip for sitting on the porch swing, sipping spiked lemonade, and listening to the birds sing. Or at least mine would.

For similar reasons, I do my damnedest to keep a clean desk. Sure, every afternoon my children deposit miscellaneous odds and ends on it, such as empty pretzel bag wrappers, finger puppets, and hair barrettes, but I make a point to clear all the debris before I hunker down for a day of writing or interviews. My intensity is easily thwarted when my attention is drawn to errant cracker crumbs and broken crayons!

Not all distractions can—or should—be avoided, such as letting my dogs out to fertilize the yard. But avoidable work interferences are the reason I often take myself out to lunch for a change of scenery while my girls are in school or with a sitter. Sometimes I need a creatively inspirational atmosphere that doesn't include beds begging to be made and dishes waiting to be stacked. It's a lot easier to block out miscellaneous chatter from people I don't know! Home life is also a hectic life, which isn't always the perfect forum for productivity.

Another thing not everyone realizes is that a work-from-home mom's flexibility is often unintentionally taken for granted. Because we're at home all day, it's hard for other folks (this may or may not include one's spouse—thankfully, mine is super laid-back on this front) to comprehend why we can't find time to squeeze in a dry cleaning drop-off or scrub the bathtub. We forgot to pull the pork chops out of the freezer? What the hell were we so busy *doing* all day long?

The truth is, a work-from-home mom has to put blinders on. We have to shut out all potential preoccupations and work at the expense of any household responsibilities. Which makes it even more complicated when, for example, one of our children comes down with the funk. We're automatic caretakers when our kids get sick—which, for the record, I wouldn't change if someone paid me! Plus, it makes total sense. Why would my husband take personal or unpaid vacation days from work when I'm already at home? I don't have to worry about getting the boss's okay, so I'm the obvious choice. But the fact remains, my work schedule is profoundly affected during school holidays and breaks, each time an air conditioning technician or plumber has to make a repair, whenever my dogs have to see the vet or be let outside to do their business, and every time one of my girls runs a fever or has a doctor appointment.

Who you gonna call? Work-from-home mama.

Office space.

Depending on your situation, you may be going to work by choice or out of necessity. Let it be said, I respect your selflessness, discipline, and achievements either way. Since when is an office equivalent to a beach in Bali? No working mom I know sits in rush hour traffic to head to a job where she can kick off her heels, lay back in a recliner, and flag down cabana boys to hand-feed her grapes. Most bosses aren't big on midmorning siestas or skipping meetings in lieu of a hot stone massage.

Going to the office isn't a vacation just because a mom is no longer at home handling laundry duties, tripping over magnetized alphabet letters, or begging kids to take a nap. So the next time someone tries to convince you work is a paid vacation, remind him your office doesn't serve pink umbrella-garnished liquid lunches! Unless, of course, you work at a bar, in which case my sympathy is on the sabbatical I'm too busy to take.

The "Business" of Being a Working Mom

I enjoy being a businesswoman and making things happen; I'm a true lover of business and the arts. Being a professional is a long-cherished passion and priority I developed not only before I had kids but back when I was still a kid myself! In fact, I'm proud to say I incorporated at the ripe old age of fifteen. To put that in perspective, I was running my company before I had my learner's permit.

In many ways, my early career prepared me for parenting. It taught me to appreciate the small details, get back up when I fall, and hear the word *no* a lot.

When I first began my career as an actress, someone told me, "They don't call it show *business* for nothing." I couldn't agree more. While there are some undeniably glamorous aspects of being an actress on a popular television series, it's still a vocation. As with any other source of employment, it calls for dedication and professionalism. And because my passion for acting runs deep, I take all aspects of it seriously—I play hard; I work hard.

The same can be said for my parenting. While I certainly don't view motherhood as a business endeavor, it sometimes requires a businesslike approach. I have to bring organization, prioritization, and negotiation skills to the table each day. Not to mention the people skills. Oh, the people skills! Toddlers call for people skills in spades. My kids have certainly redefined how I view my communication strategies!

I know of no other job that demands quite the same level of focus, fortitude, devotion, responsibility, creative input, and work ethic. Parenthood is both a calling and a lifework, and it's not an easy paycheck! As a matter of fact, there's no paycheck at all. Or potential promotion. Or pension plan. Or stock options. But on a good note, you'll never have to worry about being laid off. The only pink slips you'll be seeing are the kind that'll line your daughter's future prom dress.

Never can say good-bye.

Being a working mom comes with an abundance of common misconceptions. I once overheard Mom One say to Mom Two, "It must be so nice to get away from the rugrats each day to go to work, huh?"

Mom One was clearly in need of a babysitter. And a date night. And maybe some sex. Anyone who's under the impression it's a relief to go to work in order to "get away" from their hectic home life is only right a small portion of the time. I won't lie, there have been a smattering of days when it has been nice to leave behind the spills, stains, fusses, and freak-outs and focus on something I can actually control—like telling jokes that make an audience laugh or memorizing script pages. After all, scripts don't have meltdowns in the parking lot of the Piggly Wiggly. But that doesn't mean I don't spend the rest of the time missing my kids more than I miss fitting into my favorite pair of skinny jeans! And believe me, I miss those *a lot.* Just ask my bathroom scale.

Though I'm head over heels for my career, I'm also head over heels for my babies, and I don't relish missing time with them. Just because my kids sometimes drive me up the proverbial wall doesn't mean I want to be away from them. I'm hooked on their brand of crazy like it's the latest season of *Bachelor in Paradise*. My kids tend to be the problem *and* the solution to my rough days. They're the cause of my chaos as well as the cure. Isn't that wonderfully oxymoronic?

I don't care *how* much you adore your job. Whether you're tallying numbers, sending faxes, making cold calls, cutting hair, painting nails, delivering mail, serving salads, selling real estate, suturing cats, or whatever else is on the daily agenda, no mom enjoys waving good-bye to her heart each day. And that's what our children are—our hearts walking around outside our bodies. Or, depending on how hyper they are, our hearts skipping, hopping, running, or galloping around outside our bodies.

There's certainly validation in making a work deadline, receiving praise from a satisfied client, or closing a deal. But that doesn't diminish the agony of leaving your kids behind when you head into work! There's no place like home. Cue the Munchkins and famed ruby slippers.

Profit and loss statements.

Leaving your kids won't be the only unfortunate side effect of being a working mom. Here's a biggie—tact is tragically elusive. You may discover, if you haven't already, that some people have as much control over their tact filter as someone with Tourette syndrome might have over swearing in public. At some inopportune moment, some foolish person will affect a bogus expression of understanding and tell you how difficult it must be to "have someone else raise your kids because you're so busy pursuing your career." I call bullshit on their fake-ass attempt to commiserate.

First off, you may or may not have a choice whether to work.

Either way, that comment insinuates that you put your work before your children and that you're allowing someone else to teach them crucial life lessons because you no longer have any time to devote to doing so. This idea makes my blood boil. Just because you're a working mom doesn't mean your kids aren't your priority. Being a good mom and having a career are not mutually exclusive. You know that; I know that; hopefully someday the crazy-makers will stop perpetuating the myth.

Also in the Tact Is Harder to Find Than the Lost City of Atlantis category is the comment "You should quit your job! The time you have with your kids is worth more than all the money in the world." A good and thoughtful sentiment, sure, but not entirely true . . . Tiny humans will empty your wallet faster than J Lo on a shopping spree.

I love my kids. I love spending time with my kids. It would be awesome if I got paid to enjoy spending time with my kids. But since that whole money-makes-the-world-go-'round-but-it-doesn't-grow-on-trees thing is a very real deal for most of us, work is a foregone conclusion. It's phenomenal when we can make a living doing something we wholeheartedly love, but the money must be made no matter how you spin it. Because someday those same kids will be begging you to pay for the iPhone 24 and their latest boy-band tattoo.

Outside of a few tasteless comments and lamentable scenarios, there are some serious perks to following your career path, despite the challenges with juggling your work and home life. Having an occupation you prize offers validation and independence. After all, unlike the tasks you do as requested by your toddler, when you finish a work project, someone actually takes notice! You might even get a thank-you. How bonkers is *that*? Work forces you to take a shower, brush your hair, and get dressed each day, and during bathroom breaks at work, no one pounds on the door to ask you for the thousandth time why you won't let them have a candy bar for lunch. You can even participate in conversations that don't revolve around Big Bird and boogers. A working mom gets to put her talents to good use, reap the benefits of pursuing her passion, have daily feelings of accomplishment and adult interaction (never a bad thing), and teach her children the importance of doing so. And isn't our main goal as moms to be a good role model for our children? Career moms promote work ethic and self-esteem by instilling a love for what they do.

With all that said, I'll admit it sucks that an office job doesn't allow for pairing sweatpants with a suit jacket.

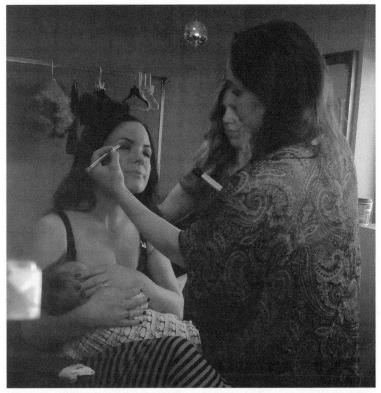

Marlowe squeezes in a snack while I have my makeup done for the first *Situation Momedy* cover shoot. *Photo courtesy of Jenna von Oy.*

Fear and self-loathing in my livelihood.

As working moms, we'll always fear those instances when we have to choose between our sick child and a career-defining meeting. And we'll always worry admitting that fear opens us up to judgment—whether it pertains to our motherly instincts or our business acumen. But in some sense, isn't that a good problem to have? It means we're providing for our children in every possible way. Someday, with any luck, our children will understand that too.

When I went back to work after having Marlowe, I didn't feel I'd spent enough time simply loving on my new baby without the distraction of book deadlines and show schedules. But you know what else? My time away from work had felt like eons. I missed it terribly, and I jumped at the opportunity to film a movie. My mom was kind enough to come to work with me to care for Marlowe in my dressing room, and thankfully Marlowe was far less afflicted by separation anxiety than Gray had been as an infant. Both of those facts made the transition an easier one.

Still, they didn't make me feel any less conflicted about the situation. Marlowe still had moments when no one could satisfy her but her mama. I could hear my kid screaming all the way out on set. As luck would have it, it was always right smack-dab in the middle of my lines. I pride myself on never breaking character while the camera is rolling, but come on! Hearing my baby call for me made me feel incredibly guilty.

It's complicated to go back to work after having children—no matter what age they are and no matter what line of work you're in. Yes, my girls are past any separation anxiety, adore their school program and babysitters, understand I'll be returning home later, and appear to be adjusting well, but that doesn't mean my heart aches any less. Nevertheless, not a day goes by that I don't feel lucky to be able to make a living doing a job I love. And not a day goes by that I don't thank God for my children.

Being a working mom is challenging; there's no denying that. But it's worth every bit of extra effort to have that much love and passion in my life. Having children reinvented what success looks like for me on a daily basis, but it also motivated me and instilled even more passion in me than I had before.

The Supply and Demand of Love

As moms, we all struggle in one way or another. We're all consumed by the need to give ample time to other responsibilities and passions, while still being there for our children in every capacity. Some of us worry being a stay-at-home mom automatically makes others think we're unqualified for careers or incapable of finding work. Some of us struggle with the idea that giving focus to our careers somehow suggests we're inattentive parents. Still others are plagued with the notion that merely mentioning the challenges of balancing work and kids implies we're ungrateful for our children. We deserve to receive the benefit of the doubt . . . and to give it too! Give mommy peer love; get mommy peer love.

THE MORAL OF MY STORY

Some days, the walls will feel like they're closing in—whether you spend them in an office or wiping down high chair trays. Keep your chin up! It doesn't matter if you're a full-time, part-time, work-from-home, or stay-at-home mom. As long as you're a trying-the-best-you-can mom, you're a good one! Case closed.

Brad, Gray, Marlowe, and me. Need I say more?
Photo courtesy of Micah Schweinsberg.

CHAPTER 12

All You Need Is More Love

A SCENIC VIEW OF MY PAST

When asked how I met my husband, Brad, I generally offer the CliffsNotes version. Don't get excited. Luck isn't on your side today.

As the song goes, "Love is a many-splendored thing." It's also a many-fucked-up thing, full of baffling courtships that teach you what you don't want (the excruciatingly hard way), anticlimactic nights spent waiting for some bozo to ring your phone like he promised to, and the occasional breakup via e-mail or text. Which, as we all know, is the honorable thing to do when faced with the option of (1) letting someone down gently, versus (2) dumping them like a totaled car. I'm not sure how or when it became standard to eschew someone's marital dreams via a method devoid of any feeling or R-E-S-P-E-C-T, but I'm not a fan. Go ahead and turn me down like a dog-eared page of *Catcher in the Rye*, but do it in person, dammit!

I digress.

Sometimes the quest for love also involves fun things such as an unexpected and terrifying foray back into the dating scene, crazy ex-girlfriends who make you consider enrolling in the Witness Protection Program, blind dates with wackadoodles your best friend *swears* are good guys, awkward sexting, and a handful of kisses wasted on dudes with whiskey breath who slip you their number on cocktail napkins. But enough about my former dating life.

Thankfully, that's not the kind of story I'm about to tell you.

In 2008, a year after I moved to Tennessee, I decided to gut and remodel a home I'd purchased in a quaint, quiet little pocket of Nashville. I was fairly familiar with the area, as it's where I'd stumbled upon Rumours Wine and Art Bar—a local gem of a place, otherwise known as my *Cheers*. It was a bar where everybody knew my name, my drink order, and more about my love life (or serious lack thereof) than they probably should have. Most importantly, it was a bar I could walk home from after a few too many drinks.

Back then, that particular part of town got lost in the shuffle of Nashville's more trendy neighborhoods, but the scene has since exploded into the area and taken down my favorite mom-and-pop wine bar with it. Trendy doesn't even cover it now and, despite my intense love for this town, Nashville has a few too many drunk bachelorette party-driven pedal taverns for my taste. But that's a bitch session for another day.

One evening, after a long day of unpacking boxes in my newly renovated house, I decided to head out for a glass of wine. What's the point of having a stunning home with a fully stocked wine fridge if you can't leave it to go to a bar down the street where you have to pay twice as much for the exact same beverage? That question was meant to be rhetorical, but I'll answer it anyway. I'd spent so much time alone, unpacking at the exclusion of everything else in my life, I needed an excuse to crawl out from under my rock. Not to mention, I couldn't have located a corkscrew in that massive jumble of moving boxes if it had been equipped with a built-in tracking device. I'd collected so much shit during my time in Los Angeles, I could've outfitted a clothing boutique attached to my very own Bed Bath & Beyond outlet, next to my very own Williams-Sonoma store. Can you say *hoarder*? Lord knows I sure could. And so I went to Rumours to feed my face, my wine-besotted soul, and my desperate need to do something that didn't involve organizing drawers or putting away utensils.

When I got to my favorite spot, there was only one other patron at the bar. Ah, someone else with enough sense to come early and avoid the college crowd, aka amateur hour. I couldn't see a face behind the newspaper, but the guy had a high-octane beer and looked too comfortable not to be a regular. One of my favorite bartenders, Shannon, immediately started pouring a glass of my preferred wine. I opened a book and began reading. (Because that was back in the days when I actually had time for such indulgences.)

Suddenly, Mr. High-Octane Beer looked up from his paper. "Where have you been lately? I haven't seen you in a while."

It came out curious rather than slimy. Point one for Mr. High-Octane. I was pretty sure I'd never met—or even seen—the guy, but I'd spent many a night stumbling home from Rumours after a glass too many with my girlfriends. To be fair, anything was possible.

"I'm in the middle of moving," I told him. "I haven't made it out of my house in a week or two."

He nodded and went back to his paper.

I resumed my all-important job of sipping Syrah like there was an impending prohibition.

Shannon looked at both of us and inquired, "Have you guys met?"

"Not officially," I answered.

"Brad, meet Jenna; Jenna, meet Brad," she said.

We smiled cordially and returned to our respective reading material. And that was that . . . Or so I thought.

A few minutes later I heard, "Are you reading *Love in the Time of Cholera*?"

I looked over to see Brad eyeing the cover. Good thing we weren't tackling *Fifty Shades of Grey* in book club that month.

"You've read it?" I asked him skeptically. Because *I* was judging a book by its cover too.

"Twice," he told me. "Once in college, when it was forced upon me, and once a few years ago when I realized I'd missed something on the first go-round."

My literary-loving heart swelled with intrigue. Most guys wouldn't touch *Love in the Time of Cholera* if it had breasts, so I was impressed. Suddenly, I noticed how good-looking the guy was. He had dimples, bright blue eyes, and an honest smile. Whatever the heck *that* means. And so began a three-hour discussion about books and grammar. My kind of fellow.

At the end of our evening, when neither of us could afford to loiter anymore without it getting weird (and without one or both of us getting drunk), we bid farewell with a loose agreement to meet back at Rumours on Friday. In other words, we made a date that didn't require doling out my phone number to a virtual stranger. It was perfect.

That Friday saw me plucking clothes from the racks of my just-organized wardrobe like a pig rooting for truffles in the South of France. There were unidentified flying undergarments, blouses colliding with bras, and skirts amassing like bodies at the morgue . . . All in an attempt to find the appropriate outfit for my pseudodate. After all, it takes a lot of effort to look effortless.

I finally made it to Rumours, waved to Shannon, and took my place at the bar. Ten minutes went by, then twenty. I silently praised my own forethought and pulled reading material out of my bag. In fact, it was the very same book that had gotten me into this mess in the first place.

"It doesn't look like our friend is coming tonight," Shannon offered once an uncomfortable amount of time had passed. I shrugged as if it weren't a big deal. Inside, I was disappointed—if *disappointed* really means shattered and embarrassed. I really thought my instincts were better. He'd struck me as stand-up guy; nothing about him had screamed *player* or *flake*.

Then again, sitting alone at that bar was screaming loudly enough to drown out my prior assessment. What had I expected? Meeting a guy at a bar is like meeting on a dating website. What you see isn't always what you get. You might accept a date with a guy who claims to be a six-foot-tall doctor with a house at the beach, and in walks a five-foot-tall candy striper with a sandpit in his backyard. Such is the life of a single gal who wears her heart on her sleeve.

So much for my love connection. I pictured game show host Chuck Woolery shaking his head in mock sympathy.

After taking the last sip of my drink, I bookmarked my novel and left to meet some friends for dinner instead. After all, why let a perfectly good outfit go to waste?

Our boy-meets-girl saga took a two-week hiatus while I nursed my wounded pride and steered clear of the bar where I'd been so shamefully left at the wine altar. But it takes a lot of discipline to stay away from a place where you get extra-large pours! Before you know it, my mom came to town, and we found ourselves at Rumours enjoying drinks and appetizers, despite my still-bruised ego. What were the chances we'd run into him anyway? Just in case, I'd changed out of my sweatpants and thrown on a little mascara.

Go figure, we were in midconversation when Mr. High-Octane came barreling through the door at breakneck speed and made a beeline for me. Evidently we had a do-not-pass-go, do-not-collect-$200, do-not-order-a-brew-or-speak-to-the-bartender kind of emergency on our hands.

My mother and I looked on in astonishment as he began some impressive groveling. The story goes: he'd closed his eyes for a few minutes to escape a rough workweek. He wound up sleeping right through the alarm he'd set for our rendezvous and woke up just shy of midnight, cursing himself for blowing it.

I wouldn't have believed the excuse if it weren't so pitiful. I mean, surely someone *that* well read could manage to come up with something more charming than "I fell asleep." Mr. High-Octane was slowly working his way toward being Brad. Not to mention, working his way back into my heart.

"I know you don't know me well enough to believe a word I'm saying," he told me, "but I hope you'll let me make it up to you. You'll never know how horrible I feel about this."

I was speechless until I wasn't. What I meant to say was, *Thank you for the apology.* Instead, I blurted out, "This is my mom." It was a lame follow-up to the poor guy's heartfelt mea culpa. He turned redder than a stop sign as he greeted his future mother-in-law.

That's when my mom realized she'd been watching the scene unfold like a particularly outrageous episode of *Montel Williams.* "I'm just going to . . . go to the bathroom," she said, suddenly excusing herself.

While she was gone, I officially accepted Brad's apology and assessed my next move. Was I supposed to invite him to join us? He made the decision for me. When my mom returned, Brad graciously thanked her for allowing him to interrupt our evening, then said good-bye and turned toward the door.

"You're leaving?" I asked in confusion. "Didn't you come in for a beer?"

"No," he responded. "I've done what I came to do; I drove over to talk to you. I didn't want to presume it was okay to ask around for your phone number, so I made all the bartenders promise to text me the next time you came in. I wanted you to hear this face-to-face; I wanted you to know how much I meant it." We watched in disbelief as he walked out.

When the door swung shut, my mom launched into a torrent of questions that sounded like she was conducting an interview for TMZ. "Did you forgive him? Why didn't you tell me he was so handsome? Did he ask you out again?"

My head was buzzing on wine and apologies; I couldn't think straight. "He didn't ask me out," I said.

"He was probably worried you'd turn him down after what he did," my mother offered.

"I had half a mind to ask *him* out," I told her," but that's not the way it's supposed to work."

"There's no such thing as *a way it's supposed to work*, Jenna," my mom said in exasperation. "What are you waiting for? Go catch him!"

I ran out the door before I lost my nerve, making a mad dash for the parking lot. He was backing up his car. "I just have a quick question," I called out breathlessly. "I'm headed to Los Angeles for a few weeks for work but . . . hypothetically, if I were to ask you out when I return, what would you say?"

He wasted no time answering. "Hypothetically, I'd look forward to it. And," he added ruefully, "I would promise not to stand you up." In the romantic-comedy version of our meet cute (starring Zooey Deschanel and Matt Damon), I couldn't have scripted it better.

Satisfied, I gave a little wave and watched my husband-to-be pull away with a huge smile on his face. Glancing at me in his rearview mirror, he waved back. Which is when my fancy heels and coordination failed me, and I promptly busted my ass right there in that gravel parking lot. I returned to my mother with bloody knees, hair askew, and the exciting news of my upcoming date with the man formerly known as Mr. High-Octane.

And that's the really long, drawn-out, klutzy story of how I fell for my husband. In more ways than one.

CUT TO . . .

Falling in love with my husband was eye-opening; falling in love with my kids has been all-consuming. There's just something magical about the depth of a mother's love for her children.

How else can you explain being able to make it through a five-hour road trip while someone incessantly kicks the back of your seat?

MY CRADLE CHRONICLES

You don't need me to tell you how to love your child. I'm certain your cup runneth over with mommy love—whether you're at your wits' end or your day is more peaceful than a Buddhist meditation.

Loving our children is, hands down, the easiest part of parenting. Even when those little rascals are wreaking havoc and causing migraines that make us want to pop pain relievers like Tic Tacs. Parenting love transcends every mistake, meltdown, mess, lie, and back talk. It's innate and unconditional, even when we're confronted with those trying moments during which we don't like our tiny humans very much. And it's okay to admit those moments exist! There's nothing wrong with acknowledging there are occasions when your kids piss you off, make you want to sleep for a decade, leave you teetering on the precipice of derangement, or leave you feeling like you found your parenting license in a Cracker Jack box. Some days are simply a diaper rash on the ass of life. How's *that* for a visual about parenting?

I think it's worth mentioning we moms have our moments too. I'm sure there are times my kids think I moderately suck, and I'm guessing I'll become even more proficient at that as they inch closer to the teenage years. But despite my aptitude for overall suckiness,

I know my girls will hold a lot of love for me deep down in those beautiful hearts of theirs. *Really* deep down, where the sidewalks end and the sun don't shine. Hey, at least *I'll* know it's in there, even if they question it.

This is my way of reminding you—and myself—we are fallible. We're bound to land our kids in therapy one way or another. But as long as we're leading with love and putting our best foot forward, we're doing our job.

In honor of the laughter and the tears . . .

You Know You're the Mom of a Toddler When:

1. You can't sit down long enough to finish a meal and you find graham cracker crumb backwash in every drink you've poured yourself. Well, aside from the alcoholic ones, which you readily use as an excuse to keep refilling that tumbler.

2. Your idea of a date night is hiring a babysitter so you and your hubby can discuss this year's taxes, followed by a quick shag in the back of the minivan.

3. You find your kid practicing her alphabet letters in permanent marker on your newly painted walls and, instead of flipping out, you show her how to properly write an *A*.

4. You're totally out of touch with pop culture, but you can recite the morning lineup on Disney and Nick Jr.

5. Your refrigerator is all gussied up with stickers and crayon. And it's better decorated than your spare bedroom.

6. You've had to void checks upon discovering miscellaneous

shapes drawn on the memo and signature lines.

7. You've pretended episodes of *Dora the Explorer* were "accidentally" deleted from your TiVo so you wouldn't have to suffer through them yet again. And because if you wake up with that theme song stuck in your head for one more morning, it's going to cause you to do some exploring of your own . . . right over the edge of your sanity.

8. Someone under the age of four can one-up your skills on an iPad.

9. It seems completely normal for the bathroom door to be flung open while you're in midpee by someone insisting you need to fetch Veggie Straws and turn on *My Little Pony right this minute*!

10. You've been publicly shamed by a little someone who tells you your breath stinks and your hair looks crazy. Even though the reason you forgot to brush your own teeth and hair is due to the fact that it took twenty minutes to convince them to let you brush *their* teeth and hair.

11. Your breakfast consists of toast crust, muffin crumbs, or whatever other leftovers are still hanging around two hours after your kid has finished eating, and you consume them over the trash can like a rabid possum.

12. You've saved every preschool art project . . . even (especially) the pinecone creature that looks like it has pink eye.

13. Your skill at one-handed wine bottle opening would impress every sommelier in the Loire Valley. Well done, you magnificent mommy multitasker!

14. You've hidden in your closet to consume a chocolate bar.

15. You've stuck your hand in an oven mitt and pulled out three-day-old cheese.

16. You've answered the question "Why?" more times today than you've eaten. Or blinked. Or taken a breath.

17. You've helped "count sleeps" for every holiday, summer break, visit from Grandma, first day of school, birthday party, park excursion, ice cream shop outing, and trip to a friend's house.

18. You've rescued your child from blowing bubbles in the dog water bowl. With her mouth. After the dogs have been drinking from it. (Excuse me while I vomit a little.)

19. There are random, blurry selfies of eyebrows and nostrils on your cell phone, and you're 99 percent sure you didn't take them. Also, you're suddenly getting the message that your phone will be disabled for the next five minutes because someone tried to bypass the security features.

20. You've been inadvertently hit in the face by all manner of elbows, knees, pillows, *Llama Llama* books, yo-yos, umbrellas, colored pencils, celery sticks, Hula-Hoops, plastic sporks . . . Let's just say it would take less time to list the things you *haven't* been inadvertently hit in the face with.

The definition of *miracle*: a family selfie where everyone is smiling.
Photo courtesy of Jenna von Oy.

Thanks for the Memories

We all have our own unique ways of extending love to our children. We might shower them with affection, save every art project, quit our job so we don't miss a single moment, take endless photographs and video documentation (selfie collages are the new scrapbooking), or journal every funny anecdote. Some of us may even do all of the above. And even though it isn't possible to save time in a bottle, or even in a sippy cup, it won't stop us from trying. In motherhood, it's not always about the milestones . . . it's about the moments.

Kids say and do wei . . . . . ./////./ . . ..rd shit. For example, the punctuation in that sentence was courtesy of Marlowe climbing into my office chair and spontaneously deciding she wanted to make a book contribution. No joke. I'm not clever enough to have come up with that on my own.

Lo and behold, kids really *do* say and do the darnedest things! My girls' innate sense of comic timing is often surprising and impressive, and it certainly keeps me on my ain't-got-time-for-a-pedicure toes. I've never been terribly adept at journaling, but I try to write down as many of the memorable stories from Gray and Marlowe's toddlerhood as possible. My love for them has only grown thanks to the humorous, adorable, spirited, charming things they've said and done. As of now, most of those anecdotes revolve around Gray, since Marlowe doesn't yet have an extensive vocabulary. But I have no doubt she'll make some stellar contributions down the road. Since I can't resist sharing the wealth, here are a few of my favorites so far.

A travel tale.

One afternoon, on the way home from day care, I opted to take back roads. We were driving down a street filled with potholes when Gray declared, "Mommy, I think your car has the hiccups today!"

A tantrum-thwarting tale.

One morning, when Gray was two, we set out to satisfy a full agenda of errands. With six or seven stops to make, we were in for an exhausting day. I was already anticipating the touch-and-go scenarios my future inevitably held.

One of the errands involved buying a birthday gift for a one-year-old, so I pulled into the parking lot of a giant toy shop.

"Ooh," Gray said when she spotted the storefront, and I realized my mistake. Every parent knows not to bring their toddler to a playground or toy store on the *front* end of errands, right? Then you're forced to pry your kid away from the toys like he's a blood-sucking leech on human skin.

Apparently, my logic had temporarily left the building. Nonetheless, we were toy-store-bound. Upon entering the novelty-filled palace of playthings, Gray immediately veered toward the kitchen section, complete with elaborate, kid-compatible supplies and grocery items. There were wooden tea sets, grill sets, blenders, and mixers. I saw pretend bologna, plastic pancakes that looked so real my stomach began protesting my lack of breakfast, fake cans of tuna, baked beans, and fruit cocktail. As if that weren't enticing enough, the stoves looked more sophisticated than the one I have at home. It almost made me drop everything and whip up a soufflé.

My little foodie was in heaven and began busying herself with pots and pans. I began my search for the perfect gift for a one-year-old boy, which I'm mostly clueless about. Thankfully, we weren't in your generic, run-of-the-mill, dollhouse extravaganza. There were tons of innovative, educational options, and the perfect gift found its way into my hands in no time flat.

As the cashier wrapped the present, I watched my daughter playing happily. I started panicking over how to avoid the meltdown that was bound to ensue when I explained it was time to leave behind all the super-fun toys and embark an exciting trip to the nearest FedEx Office. But that's when my child surprised the heck out of me. "Mommy, are we ready to go yet?" she shouted across the store. "I'm hungry, and I need to go to Starbucks to get a cheese Danish."

There was scattered laughter from my fellow patrons as I breathed a sigh of relief. Leave it to my kid to inherit my Starbucks obsession by the age of two.

A tinsel tale.

During December 2015, when Gray was three, she got sick of counting down the sleeps until Christmas. On Christmas Eve, antsier than ever, she sauntered into our living room and ogled the empty space beneath our tree. "Mommy, where are all of my presents?" she asked.

"I imagine they're in Santa's sleigh," I answered.

She gasped. "Oh no! Is he sitting on them?"

A titillating tale.

When Gray was two, she asked, "Mommy, do you have pectoral muscles?"

I immediately recognized the source of her inquiry. "Have you been discussing anatomy with your dad again?"

My husband has the propensity to launch into in-depth explanations on scientific subjects that mostly go over our kids' heads. But sometimes they don't.

"Yep," she answered.

"I do, in fact, have pectoral muscles," I told her.

"No, you don't," she argued confidently. "Daddy has pectoral muscles. You have boobies."

And really, who can contest that logic?

A tattle tale.

I was washing dishes in the kitchen one afternoon when Gray called out, "Mommy, come quick! Marlowe is scrubbing the stroller wheels with your toothbrush!"

That night the trash can was the proud recipient of his very own toothbrush.

A tired tale.

As I mentioned in an earlier chapter, we read and make up stories every night before bed. The girls always come up with the subject matter, though that's sometimes a point of contention.

One night, just prior to St. Patrick's Day 2016, Gray was pondering possible story lines and finally settled on one. "Can you please tell me the story about the St. Patrick's Day leper?" she requested.

Insert a pregnant pause as I attempted to fight off the visual of a not-so-magically delicious little green guy in a top hat and elf shoes, ravaged by infection. I also resisted the urge to answer, "Is that the one where the rainbow leads to the quarantined colony instead of the pot of gold?" or "Is that the one where his shamrock falls off?" Not PC, I know, and *way* over a three-year-old's head, but . . . that's just where my wonderfully warped little brain went.

Instead, I stifled my fit of giggles, looked at Gray, and said, "I don't think that story will have quite the happy ending you were hoping for. How about I tell one about leprechauns instead?" Thankfully, she agreed.

A twisted tale.

My favorite joke Gray has ever told: "Why didn't the chicken cross the road? Because he didn't want to be scared and flattened."

A tyrannical tale.

After a ten-minute dissertation on how I should clean up a soup spill, my budding CEO told me, "I know you know how to do stuff already, Mommy, but I like to tell you how to do it anyway."

I've noticed.

A tasty tale.

When she was eighteen months old, Marlowe demonstrated

her version of an after-school snack by licking the television remote control. Apparently, she's got a taste for technology.

A toon tale.

One week, when she was three, Gray's preschool class was taught a casual lesson on politics. When I picked her up that Friday, she said, "Mommy, I think I'm going to be president of the United States someday. You know, instead of being Minnie Mouse."

A toy tale.

After what must've been an incredibly challenging time attempting to diaper and dress her favorite plush friends, Gray told me, "Mom, when I was being a mom to my stuffed animals just now, I realized how hard it actually is to be a mom!"

Yes. Yes, it is. But it's damn funny too.

THE MORAL OF MY STORY

Sometimes in life, we fall on our ass. In the dating game, the trick is getting back up again, shaking ourselves off, and smiling through skinned knees—literally and figuratively. In parenting, it's keeping our wits about us, learning as we go, and leading with love . . . even when that declaration of love is continually drowned out by tears and tantrums.

Rest assured, our toddlers will make us insane in the mom-brain from time to time. They will continue to upgrade their methods of riling, rousting, battling, nagging, incensing, and testing us. They'll surprise, scare, inspire, and impassion us. They'll teach us selflessness and the true meaning of sacrifice. They'll make us slaves to our emotions, force us to bend in ways a contortionist can only dream of, and stretch our imaginations and the bounds of our love. Parenting is a lifelong, love-filled tug of war. But you know what else parenting is? The best thing we'll ever do in this lifetime.

I recently read a quote by author Mary Anne Radmacher that said, "Courage doesn't always roar. Sometimes courage is the quiet voice at the end of the day, saying, 'I will try again tomorrow.'" That's how I view motherhood. There are days I feel brave, thick-skinned, sassy, and ready to take on whatever the universe or my kids throw at me. (Unless it's shoes. Those hurt.) Other days, I roll out of bed with sleep in my eyes and uncertainty in my soul. On those days, I fake it 'til I make it. Or, to tie in another apropos cliché, I never let them see me sweat! Especially since my toddler is likely to publicly ask why my armpit is leaky and smelly.

There's no motherhood handbook, but here's one thing I know—you're courageous for waking up with the goal of bettering a tiny human's life today, and you'll be courageous again tomorrow. Now go be the best toddler mommy you know how to be! As always, I wish you luck, love, and lots of comedy along the way.

Acknowledgments

The acknowledgments in my first book were a novel unto themselves, so I'll try to make these as short and sweet as possible. With that in mind, please forgive me if I fail to mention your contribution to this book. I promise it doesn't diminish your contribution in my heart, or the gratitude with which I received it in the first place!

As with my first book, I want to thank the following people for their help, expertise, love, support, encouragement, inspiration, and commiseration over cocktails. My husband, Brad, and our daughters, Gray and Marlowe (who, for the record, didn't partake in the aforementioned cocktails): You are the definition of love. Thank you for giving me so many wonderful memories to write about. *All the friends, family (especially Mom, Dad, Pete, Alyssa, Tyler, and Linda), and fans who read my first book, proudly purchased multiple copies, showed up to my signings, and blew up their social media pages in an effort to help me get the word out.* You're the reason there's a sequel.

The Medallion team—my editor Emily Steele, Art Director Jim Tampa, Sales and Marketing Director Brigitte Shepard, and Senior Vice President Heather Musick: Thank you for believing I could—and should—bring more funny to the table! *My literary agent, Margaret O'Connor, Manager Kelly Garner, Imperium 7 Agents Tracy Mapes and Steven Neibert, and Publicist Tej Bhatia-Herring:* For sticking with me and never blowing smoke. I love you guys for that!

My book cover photo shoot crew: Photographer Extraordinaire Brooke Boling, with help from Andres Martinez, Derrick Hood, Lorena Lopez, Neil Robison, Elise Lacret, and everyone at White Avenue Studio: For putting together an incredible shoot, and providing my girls a comfort zone in which to explore their inner comediennes. That perfect shot would never have happened without your collaboration. *Mimosa Arts and Micah Schweinsberg:* For allowing me to include some of your wonderful photos. *Robyn Rhodes:* For your supportive friendship *and* stunning cover shoot jewelry! *Sarah Price:* For hiding all the gray hairs (sorry, Gray—*white* hairs) that motherhood has bestowed upon me. *Jim Reilley and Eric Fritsch:* For helping me with a kickass audiobook and always getting my jokes.

My Inner Mommy Circle, especially Lisa Dorian, Beth Jones, Katie Palmissano, Brittany Inman, Lila McCann, and Cindy Alexander: For eagerly lending your listening ears as well as your own tales of wonder and woe. Thanks for reminding me I'm not alone in this magical motherhood madness! *My dear friend, Jenn Schott:* For all the dinners full of friendship and therapy! *My friends Justin Kopplin, JD Inman, and Kal Penn:* For letting me publicly share anecdotes from our friendship, regardless of how embarrassing they might be. *Tabitha Gould & Andrea Reed:* For the exhaustive love and care you've shown my daughters. And also for distracting them so I could find time to write a book! *Heidi at BrickTop's:* For the therapeutic conversation and glass of wine that kept me from frantically telling a crowded restaurant I'd lost half of my book manuscript. *Adam Cole:* For helping my husband navigate getting that manuscript back again!